IMAGES
of America

EARLY EAGLE

THE TOWN
OF
EAGLE
EAGLE COUNTY COLORADO.
1905

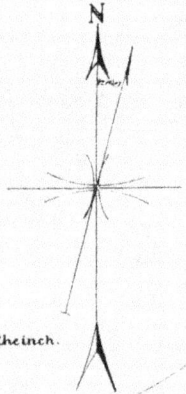

Scale: 200 F⁹ to the inch.

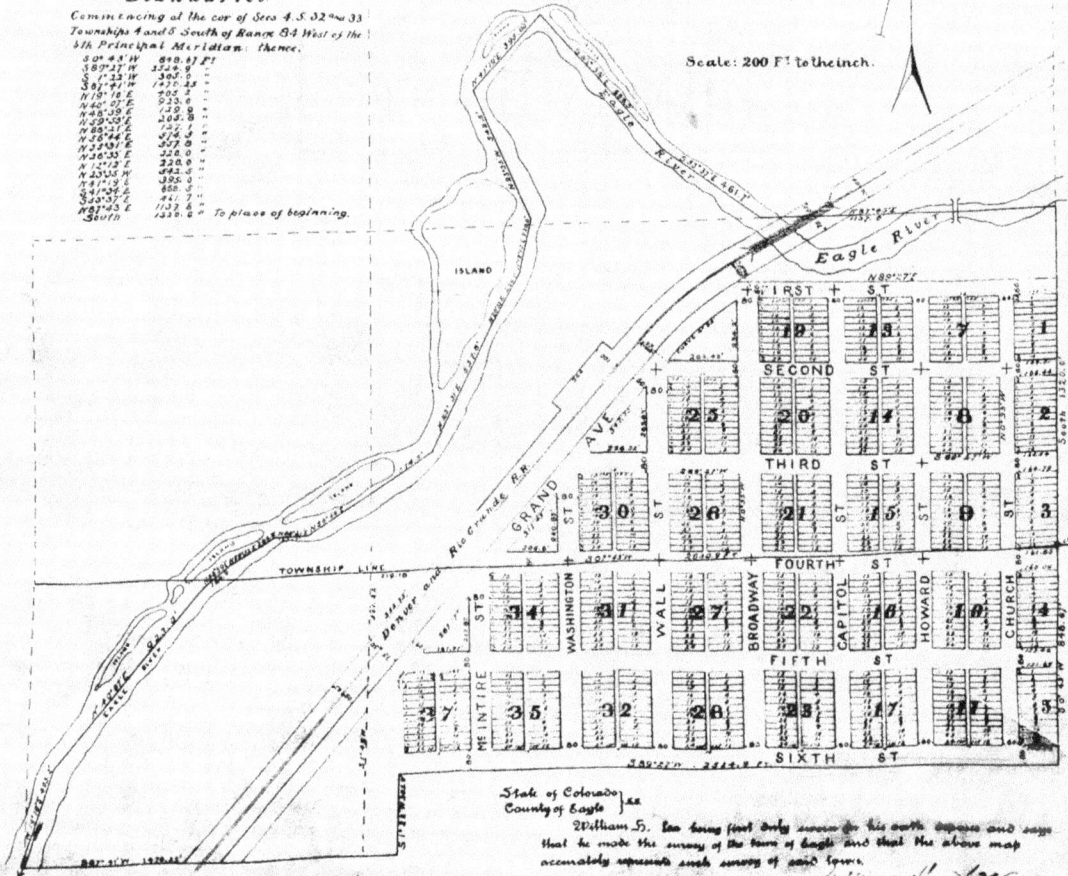

Boundaries
Commencing at the cor of Secs 4.5.32 and 33
Townships 4 and 5 South of Range 84 West of the
6th Principal Meridian: thence.

In 1905, the pioneers who came to the valley in the late 1800s decided to organize an official town. This plat map outlines the original town boundaries (these days referred to as "old-town Eagle"). Note that First Street is now Highway 6. A few years later, a brochure promoting the town described Eagle as "not the largest but the best town in Colorado." (Image edited by Mike Crabtree.)

ON THE COVER: C. F. Nogal built Eagle's first permanent hotel in 1892. The building still stands at the intersection of Highway 6 and Capitol Street. The 13-room hotel could accommodate up to 26 boarders. Water was hauled from the Eagle River, horses and wagons hauled supplies from the Red Cliff mining camp, and fuelwood was cut by hand. The O. A. Ping family purchased the hotel in 1923. (Eagle County Historical Society.)

IMAGES
of America

EARLY EAGLE

Kathy Heicher and the
Eagle County Historical Society

ARCADIA
PUBLISHING

Published by Arcadia Publishing
Charleston, South Carolina

Library of Congress Control Number: 2010920199

For all general information contact Arcadia Publishing at:
Telephone 843-853-2070
Fax 843-853-0044
E-mail sales@arcadiapublishing.com
For customer service and orders:
Toll-Free 1-888-313-2665

Visit us on the Internet at www.arcadiapublishing.com

*In memory of my parents, John and Betty Lell, who
would have been proud to see this book.*

`

CONTENTS

ACKNOWLEDGMENTS

One person alone cannot produce a local history book. It takes an entire town. This publication relies on years of work by the Eagle County Historical Society (ECHS). Much credit goes to the early leaders of that group including Laurene Knupp, Frank Doll, Jim Nimon, Jean Johnson, and Myrtie Stephens as well as many others. Thirty years ago, they recognized the need to create an Eagle County history record and volunteered countless hours and resources toward that goal. Credit also goes to the staff of the Eagle Public Library whose expertise made those collected records and ECHS photographs readily available to the public.

Special acknowledgement goes to the late Leonard Ping. A lifelong Eagle resident, Leonard was an accomplished photographer who for many years recorded the history of this community with the snap of his camera shutter. Leonard was also something of a pack rat, and apparently saved copies of just about every photograph he ever snapped. It was the generosity of his relatives Claude and Vieva DeGraw and their willingness to share those photographs that convinced me this book was a doable project.

A number of people also opened their family photograph albums and generously shared their personal history collections. Many thanks go to John Buchholz, Teresa Lewis, Peggy (Randall) Buckau, John Oleson, Bill Johnson, Debera Dice Stewart, Shirley Shelton, Alice Koonce, and Pam (McCain) Schultz and their families.

Among those who gave up their personal time to help identify photographs were George and Lena Yost, Star Doll, and Art and Helen Davenport. Professional photographer Mike Crabtree shared his edited photographs. Archaeologists Mike Metcalf and Kevin Black shared their knowledge. A chance meeting made Jerry Santoro a computer courier, which was a huge help on deadline. Local history librarian Jaci Spuhler of the Eagle Public Library helped immeasurably by conveying photographs and keeping excellent, accessible archives. Special thanks go to Jaci and my husband, Bill, for their proofreading and patience.

A message for readers: go through your photograph albums and label every image with names, places, dates, and details. Future historians will be forever grateful.

INTRODUCTION

There was a time when everybody in the little mountain town of Eagle knew one another. In fact, many people were somehow blood-related. Newcomers were teasingly advised that the population of the town basically consisted of just a couple of family lines: "the Rules, the Randalls, and the relatives."

Times have changed. The *Christian Science Monitor* officially classifies Eagle as a "boom town." With a population that has more than doubled in the past decade (55 percent of the town residents have lived here five years or less), there are more strangers than familiar faces at the post office, grocery store, and community events.

What the long-established residents and newcomers have in common is a love for the community. This book utilizes a collection of historic images and anecdotes to present a snapshot of Eagle's history. The intent is to provide a link between present-day Eagle and its past for people who love this town. Stories of pioneers like C. F. "Charley" Nogal paint a picture of how Eagle got its start and offer insight into present-day Eagle.

Charley Nogal arrived in Eagle in September 1885. The young pioneer came to the valley with little money, but plenty of vision, determination, and a sense of adventure. Those same qualities, exhibited by the "pioneers" of many different decades, have bolstered Eagle for more than a century, shaping it into the thriving mountain community that it is today. Nogal, born in Ohio in 1855, seemed destined to follow his father in the bricklaying and stonecutting business. However, even as a boy, he was fascinated by the stories of wonderful land out West. As a young man, he received a letter from a friend describing the many opportunities open to men adventurous enough to journey westward. That was all the incentive Nogal needed to change his life's direction.

Nogal headed west via train. When the train tracks ended, he continued his journey by hitching a ride in a covered wagon that he shared with six hogs. "It wasn't so bad in the daytime; but I could hardly sleep at night," he recalled many years later. That first westward journey halted for a time at Cedar Vale, Kansas, where he stayed long enough to start a ranch and marry Rosetta Metheney, a woman known for her kindness and generosity.

In Cedar Vale, Nogal met Henry Arthur Hockett, one of Eagle's earliest homesteaders. Hockett gave a glowing report of the Eagle Valley, describing it as "good farming country," healthy for both crops and families.

By the spring of 1885, Nogal was determined to push farther west. Charley, Rosetta, and their young son Edgar traveled to Red Cliff by train. Anxious to get to the country that Hockett had described, the Nogals used a hired mule, a borrowed buckboard, and horses to work their way through a spring blizzard and down the Eagle River Valley.

Eventually they arrived at the little settlement on Brush Creek, which at that time was known as "Castle." They were welcomed into the Hockett house by Hockett's gracious wife, Mary. By September, Nogal had staked out "Stone Pile 80," claiming a homestead on the Eagle River that he later declared to be "one of the finest ranches in the valley." He built a log cabin near the point where a rickety bridge crossed the Eagle River. The family survived that first difficult winter by eating game meat.

By 1886, the entrepreneurial Nogal recognized a business opportunity to serve the people who were traveling by stagecoach through the valley. He set up a wayfarer's station that consisted of several tents. Travelers could buy supplies in the store tent, eat a substantial meal for 25¢ in the restaurant tent, enjoy a drink in the saloon tent, then rest for the night at the hotel tent (the 25¢ bed price doubled if the Nogals supplied the bedding). Many of the clients were prospectors chasing reports of gold in the mountains of Brush Creek, a tributary to the Eagle River. The little community on the Eagle River was the last settlement on the way to the booming Fulford mining district.

When the Rio Grand Railroad extended tracks through the community in 1887, the work crew quartered at Nogal's "stage station." Years later, Rosetta Nogal would tell of preparing a breakfast of venison, potatoes, biscuits, fruit, and coffee for 80 men. The biscuits alone required a 50-pound sack of flour.

Reportedly, the wayfarer's station earned about $2,000 for Nogal during the first summer of operation. Nogal used some of those profits to buy a block of land (now the north end of the downtown central business district) from William Edwards and build a store. In 1889, he accepted a $20 per month job as postmaster, handling the mail out of his store.

In 1892, Nogal built the town's first permanent hotel (pictured on the cover of this book) on the corner of Capitol and First Streets. The building, aged and unused for many decades, stands today on the corner of what is now Capitol Street and Highway 6.

The Nogal family had a presence in Eagle for more than 80 years. Charley Nogal was just one of many pioneers who shaped Eagle into the community that it is today. Some were homesteaders, such as Henry Hernage. Many, like Arthur Fulford, were miners. Ranchers like John Love brought cattle to Brush Creek and cultivated crops. The politically inclined, like Nick Buchholz, stepped up to fill leadership roles while establishing needed businesses and managing homesteads.

Eagle's history stretches well beyond the town boundaries. The surrounding mesas and valleys (Eby Creek, Bellyache, Castle Peak, Brush Creek) and the mountains beyond also played a role in this community's history. Those names and events of the past (think Hockett Gulch, Nogal Road, Hernage Creek, Mayer Street) are entwined with life in Eagle today.

Eagle has weathered its share of good times and hard times. And despite the many changes, Eagle, because of its location and character, remains the kind of small town community that draws people whose dream is to live in the Colorado mountains.

Credit the many people who, like Charley Nogal, came to this valley with vision, determination, and a sense of adventure.

One

THE FIRST PEOPLE

BEFORE 1879

Eagle's human history started long before the first ambitious pioneers erected tents and built cabins along the Eagle River in the 1880s. Archaeological evidence verifies the presence of prehistoric hunter-gatherers in the region more than 10,000 years ago. By 500 years ago, archeological records (tools, food, pottery, and campsites) reveal traits of the historical living patterns of the Ute people. The earliest residents of the valley probably lived here seasonally, rather than staying year-round.

Maps from the Hayden survey in the early 1870s show the "Ute Trail," a network of prehistoric and historic trails used by early people to traverse the high plateau of the nearby Flat Tops. Early people used those trails to move about the territory roughly extending from Dotsero to Meeker, and as far north as Steamboat Springs. The Utes were one of the first groups of Native Americans to gain access to horses, which allowed them to greatly expand their territory.

Present-day archaeologists have recorded evidence of the Ute presence in the valley. In the pinion-juniper–covered hills north of Eagle lay the remains of a game fence (a sort of hedge made of entwined branches) used to influence the movement of deer and elk toward waiting hunters. The remains of primitive *wickiups* (a temporary, ground-surface shelter built with woven mats of branches and brush) have been noted in the hills around Brush Creek. Other significant finds in the region include eagle traps, rock art, vision quest sites, arrow points, and other tools. Anthills on mesas near Eagle occasionally yield tiny trade beads from long ago.

Newspaper archives and other historic accounts dating to the early 1880s tell stories of trappers and miners encountering bands of Utes camped on Brush Creek. The Utes were not receptive to intrusions, which kept the newcomers wary.

There is no official historic record in the Eagle County archives of the Ute people being removed from this area. However, by the early 1880s various political policies and treaties were used to move the Native Americans out of their historic territory and onto reservations. The removal of the Utes cleared the way for the homesteaders and miners to come into the valley, starting a new era for Eagle.

This photograph, snapped in the 1920s near Eagle, shows a wickiup, likely built by the Ute people. Notes accompanying the image suggest the location is on what was once the Macdonell ranch, located on lower Brush Creek. Used seasonally, the primitive shelter, which probably dates back to the 1860s–1870s, featured woven branches of pinion and juniper to create a structure that would shed some water. The woman posing inside the wickiup is believed to be Mary Hannah Buchholz Gamble (Johnston), along with an unidentified child. Local ranchers in the 1920s and 1930s reported finding primitive shelters and other signs of a Ute presence in areas such as the "Three Sisters" mountain formation on Brush Creek. Archaeologists have also recorded finds in the region that include eagle traps, game fences, and rock art. At one time, many local residents had their own collections of arrowheads and primitive tools. (ECHS; Ping-DeGraw Collection.)

In addition to documented artifacts, there are a few stories (or possibly legends) of the Ute presence in the Eagle area recorded in local history archives. John Root, a trapper, claimed that while working in the Eagle area in the late 1860s, he and fellow trappers were confronted by Utes who confiscated two otter hides. The trappers were taken to a Ute camp located near what is now the Eagle cemetery, where they met with Chief Colorow (pictured). Colorow ordered the trappers to leave the Brush Creek Valley. The men packed up their traps and walked east along the Eagle River to the mouth of Lake Creek, where they camped for the remainder of the winter. George Bowland, a pioneer of Eagle County, wrote in his memoir of miners being turned away from Brush Creek by the Utes in 1879–1880. A history written by local schoolchildren in the 1940s mentions the remnants of a Ute horse racing track on the Sproule ranch on lower Brush Creek. (Denver Public Library, Western History Collection, Z-166.)

The most reliable record of the presence of the Ute people in the Eagle region comes from a variety of archeological investigations over the years. Ute activity was more intense in the Colorado River Basin, north of Eagle, than along the Eagle River Valley and its tributaries. Pictured above is the crew of Eagle-based Metcalf Archaeological Consultants exploring a site along the Colorado River (approximately 21 miles northeast of Eagle) in 1987. That survey yielded evidence of a prehistoric Ute culture, including pit houses and campfires, dating back as far as 6,500 years. Among the archeological finds that have been recorded in the valley are a 250-foot-long "game fence" made of tangled branches and shrubbery, an "eagle trap" (a cone of stacked rocks on a crag high above the Colorado River), and possible burial platforms. Historic records indicate the last observation of free Ute people in the valley may have been in 1880, the year after the Meeker massacre. Brush Creek prospector Jack Layton claimed to have seen Ute people fleeing the valley. (Kevin Black.)

Two

THE SETTLEMENT ON BRUSH CREEK
1880–1904

In the early days, the community that formed at the junction of Brush Creek and the Eagle River suffered something of an identity crisis.

While men seeking gold and silver were drawn up Brush Creek to the mining boomtown of Fulford, others recognized riches of another sort in the fertile soils and plentiful water of the Brush Creek Valley. In 1887, William Edwards claimed 156 acres at the mouth of Brush Creek and laid out a town site that he called "Castle"—probably a reference to the prominent landmark of Castle Peak to the north.

When the Rio Grande Railroad arrived in the late 1880s, the railroad company named its new station "Rio Aquilla," Spanish for "Eagle River." For a brief period of time, the formative little community was also called "Brush." An 1890 Colorado business directory lists the name of the settlement as "Eagle River Crossing" and counts the population at 25 residents.

In 1892, A. A. McDonald purchased the town site for back taxes, and renamed the little settlement after himself. However "McDonald" never caught on with the locals. By 1896, McDonald gave up on his real estate adventure, and the community's name was changed to "Eagle," reportedly a name handed down from the first trappers in the valley.

By 1900, the community claimed a population of 124; however, the May 24, 1901, edition of the *Eagle Valley Enterprise* newspaper estimated that several hundred people lived within a 1-mile radius of the settlement. The community boasted a newspaper, three general stores, two large halls, a school building, a hotel, a saloon, a meat market, a carpenter shop, a harness maker and repair business, and a first class barbershop. The Hadley brothers operated a stage line between Eagle and the mining camp of Fulford on East Brush Creek. Agriculture was fast emerging as a solid economic force.

"Blessed with many natural advantages and with an era of homebuilding now well underway, who shall say that the future of the Eagle Valley is not assured most favorably?" asked the *Enterprise* on May 24, 1901.

This 1884 photograph is believed to show the first home in Eagle, located about a half mile south of the mouth of Brush Creek in what is now the Eagle Ranch subdivision. (View is to the west.) Pictured are Martha Taunton Goodall (standing) and Sarah Alice Goodall Wood (feeding the fawn). William F. Wood and Henry C. Goodall sit in the wagon. Sarah Alice was 14 years old when she married William in a ceremony that took place in the cabin, according to family archives. Other than this photograph, there is little record of the Goodall and Wood families during their time in Eagle. Homesteaders began to flock to Eagle in the early 1880s, drawn both by stories of rich ore veins in the Fulford Mining District (on East Brush Creek) and by the fertile farming land and abundant water in the valley. (ECHS; Griffiths Family Collection, edited by Mike Crabtree.)

The first person to be buried in what is now the Sunset View Cemetery in Eagle was Lizzie Hernage, who died tragically at the age of 24. Lizzie was the wife of Henry J. Hernage, an Englishman who came to Brush Creek in the early 1880s. He was a stock grower and homesteader who at one time, together with Webb Frost, controlled vast quantities of land on Brush Creek before formal homestead claims were filed. On July 29, 1885, Henry and Lizzie were moving a herd of cattle across a rickety bridge over the Eagle River. The bridge collapsed, and Lizzie drowned. Henry gave up his claim on Brush Creek not long after and moved to Yampa, where he owned and operated the very successful Hernage Mercantile Company. In the photograph below, author Kathy Heicher explores the original homestead on Hernage Creek (south of the Eagle Ranch subdivision). (Kathy and Bill Heicher.)

Pioneer Nicholas (Nick) Buchholz, an immigrant from Germany, served with honor in the Confederate army. He was engaged in the mercantile and butcher business in Maryland, Virginia, and Washington, D.C., before making his way west with his family in 1882. Nick and his wife, Mary, homesteaded 640 acres on a mesa north of town (now the Highlands Meadows subdivision). The first winter was difficult. Confined in their cabins for weeks by unrelenting snow and bitter cold temperatures, many settlers ran out of flour and survived on a diet of vegetables and venison. In 1889, Nick was the first rancher to bring sheep into the county. He abandoned sheep ranching after coming up against strong opposition from local cattlemen who did not want sheep on grazing lands. Buchholz's son John and daughter Hannah later homesteaded another 640 acres higher up on Castle Peak ("Buchholz Mesa"). That land is still held by the Buchholz family. Standing are, from left to right, Nick, daughter Bertha, wife Mary, unknown, unknown, and Leo Buchholz. (ECHS; Buchholz Family Collection.)

Nick and Mary Buchholz sit on the rock surrounded by their children. The children are, from left to right, Bertha (who died at a young age), Jim (standing), John, Hannah, and Leo (sitting). For many years, the Nick Buchholz family played a prominent role in Eagle's history. A devout Catholic, Nick was a driving force in the establishment of St. Mary's Catholic Church in Eagle, and he worked hard to establish quality public schools in the valley. He was also a shrewd politician and ardent democrat who served for many years as the Eagle County assessor. (See Chapter 3, pages 38 and 39). (ECHS; Buchholz Family Collection.)

Mary O. Adams (Buchholz) was a niece of U.S. president John Quincy Adams. She grew up on the Adams family plantation near Virginia City, Virginia, that was destroyed during the Civil War. In 1866, she married Nick Buchholz, who had served with Mosby's famous "Black Horse Troop" in the Confederate army. In 1881, the Buchholzes and their five children came to Leadville with the intent of mining for silver. However, by the time they reached Leadville, the silver boom had busted. Nick found work burning charcoal for the mine smelters. From Leadville, the Buchholzes moved to Red Cliff, then down the valley to Eagle where they remained for the rest of their lives. Like many pioneer women, Mary was as capable as her husband in ranching cattle, growing crops, and raising children. She died in 1903 at the age of 61. (ECHS; Buchholz Family Collection.)

"Humble" would be an apt description of the structures that Eagle pioneers used as homes in the late 1880s. The Homestead Act of 1862 allowed any U.S. citizen over the age of 21 to claim 160 acres of surveyed public land after five years of continuous residence on the property and payment of a modest ($26 to $34) registration fee. That ability to acquire land was the draw that brought many pioneers to Eagle. The crumbling remains of many of these homestead cabins are still in evidence in various draws and hills around Eagle. The sod-roofed structure above was likely located on Bellyache Mountain (on property that is now part of the Diamond S Ranch). The dirt roof provided insulation from both heat and cold. The cabin in the trees appears to be located east of town on the Eagle River, possibly referred to as the "Edwards place." (ECHS's Ping-DeGraw Collection.)

Dave and Jennie Abrams homesteaded on land 4 miles southwest of Eagle (Abrams Creek) in the fall of 1882. Originally from Philadelphia, the Abramses traveled by wagon from Red Cliff down the Eagle River Valley to Squaw Creek. From there, they followed a stage road to Brush Creek. They raised seven children on their homestead. In addition to raising some stock and growing some crops, the family located and worked a copper mine near their home. When the mine proved unproductive, they moved down to the edge of the Brush Creek Valley where they built another home. There are two graves on the original Abrams homestead, believed to be those of Dave and his oldest son, Abe. Stories about those deaths suggest that violence within the family may have been a factor. The haying photograph below appears to have been taken on Brush Creek (view is to the northeast). (ECHS; Abrams Family Collection.)

The Barclay Hocketts, a Quaker family that included five children, moved to Eagle from Indiana in 1882, homesteading in a one-and-a-half-story cabin at the mouth of Brush Creek. The pioneers socialized regularly, and early day newspapers carry reports of dances being held at the cabin. Space was limited, so men without partners had to stand outside the cabin while the reels and waltzes were danced. All three Hockett sons, Henry Arthur ("Art"), Sylvester, and Addison, took up adjacent homesteads. Addison brought a sawmill to Hardscrabble Mountain during the 1890s and operated it until the turn of the century. Pictured above is Barclay's son Art Hockett, his wife Mary, and their daughter Perie in 1895. In 1908, Art was one of the first Brush Creek ranchers to be issued a Forest Service grazing permit. Perie Hockett, who married John Green, died in the 1918 Spanish flu epidemic. (ECHS.)

Myrtie Hockett Gant, pictured in this 1895 portrait, was one of the twin daughters of Barclay Hockett. The family's first winter on Brush Creek in 1883 was one of hardship. Snowed into their cabin, the family survived by eating turnips. Social event reports in the newspaper indicate that Myrtie and her twin sister, Minnie, were popular at dances on Brush Creek. (ECHS.)

Art and Mary Hockett eventually left their homestead cabin and built this elegant Victorian-style home in town. The house still stands on the southwest corner of Second and Howard Streets. (Photograph dates to the 1920s.) The Hockett family eventually moved to Gypsum, where they took up ranching. (ECHS.)

William Edwards claimed 156 acres at the mouth of Brush Creek in 1887 and laid out a town site called "Castle." The first business establishment was a general merchandise store, housed in a tent. Pioneer C. F. "Charley" Nogal purchased a square block of land in the town site from Edwards in 1888. He operated a "stage station" consisting of several businesses including a hotel, restaurant, and saloon that initially operated out of tents. Nogal reportedly made an impressive $2,000 in profits that first summer by allowing two stage routes (Glenwood Springs and Minturn) to headquarter out of his complex. With the profit he made in the first year of operation, Nogal built a more permanent store building. Frustrated by customers who failed to pay their bills, he eventually sold the store to Ralph Belding. This photograph was found in the Ping collection, stored in the Nogal hotel building pictured on the cover. (ECHS; Ping-DeGraw Collection.)

Charley Nogal and his wife, Rosetta, arrived in 1885, claiming a homestead on what is now the Eagle River Villas housing complex, north of the Eagle River. Like most homesteaders, their first home was a modest cabin, reportedly built with logs taken from the remains of the first bridge over the river. They constructed their second home (pictured above) in 1905. The original Nogal house has since been moved a short distance to the west and is now the Eagle River Anglers store. In the photograph at left, Charley and Rosetta Nogal pose on their 50th wedding anniversary in 1930. Charley, who lived to be 92 (dying in 1948), walked to town every day to pick up his mail and buy a cigar. Rosetta died in 1940. (ECHS.)

By 1895, the settlement on Brush Creek (then named "McDonald") was beginning to take the shape of a community. The original tent "buildings" and sod-roofed shelters were giving way to more permanent structures built of logs, wood, and bricks. The pioneers who came to explore the valley recognized the agricultural potential of the Brush Creek Valley, while the prospectors seeking gold were drawn by reports of rich ore veins up Brush Creek. A. A. McDonald, the man who owned most of the land in the settlement at the time, built the canvas-roofed structure on the far left as a hall for the Fourth of July celebration. The view in this photograph is northwest, toward Eby Creek Mesa. (ECHS.)

Horses and wagons were the primary mode of transportation in the early days. People relied on wagons to haul materials to homesteads, for transportation between settlements, and to ferry items from the railroad to ranches and businesses. Originally, the primary road from Red Cliff to Eagle was a route that started over Bellyache Mountain at Squaw Creek, and ended in the Brush Creek Valley (Trail Gulch). That road still exists. A road down through the Eagle River Valley was completed in 1887, which shifted the travel corridor away from the Brush Creek Valley. In both of these photographs, the wagons are in Eagle, likely on what was at one time First Street (now Highway 6). The Nogal hotel can be seen in the background. (ECHS; Ping-DeGraw Collection.)

Harvey Dice and his brother Thomas constructed the "Dice Building" on the west side of Broadway in 1904. The cost of the original building was $1,505. The first occupants were a saloon, the "Pony Resort," operated by Wolcott resident Jack Hall; and the "Silver Eagle Tonsorial Parlor," a barbershop and bath operated by Grant Holton. Miners coming into town on a Saturday night paid 25¢ for a bath. A shave and a haircut cost six bits (75¢). The street-level space had several uses over the next couple of decades, including a post office and a drugstore with a soda fountain. The upper floors of the building were used for a variety of business and professional offices, as well as for residential quarters. Local lawyers Gene and Bill Luby and Hume White at varying times ran their law practices from the building. In recent years, restaurants have occupied it. (ECHS.)

Saloons came to Eagle along with the homesteaders and the miners. The first tenant of the Dice Building in 1904 was the Pony Resort, a saloon and poolroom. C. S. Lumley operated the Eagle Club (which featured a musical slot machine) in the brick building around the corner on Second Street. Another saloon was called the "Bucket of Blood." Brothers Byron and Charles Zartman purchased the Eagle Club and operated it until 1918. Lumley later opened another establishment,

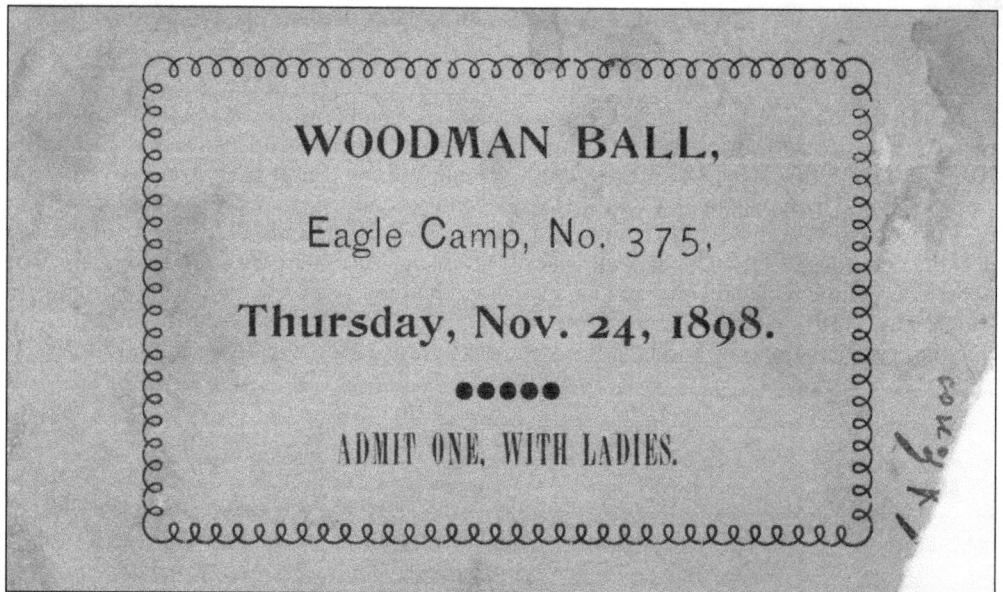

WOODMAN BALL,

Eagle Camp, No. 375,

Thursday, Nov. 24, 1898.

●●●●●

ADMIT ONE, WITH LADIES.

The Woodmen of the World fraternal organization built the Woodman Hall on Eagle's main street in 1897 (currently the site of the Brush Creek Saloon). Originally one story, the building was expanded in 1911. For many years the Woodman Hall was the center of social life in Eagle. (Randall family collection; Peggy Buckau.)

the Log Cabin Saloon, where Zangs famous beer was always on tap. He also offered several whiskey brands, including Yellowstone, Sam Clay, and Old Forester, along with Marguerite cigars. The name of the saloon in the picture is not known. Note the spittoons at strategic locations on the floor and the complete absence of women (although dogs apparently were allowed). (Buchholz Family Collection.)

Peter and Caroline Thoberg came to the Eagle Valley in 1885 to ranch. They settled on property east of town, which they developed from a rough sagebrush flat into a splendid productive ranch. In 1904, they moved into town. Peter served on the first town board. Caroline was a charter member of the Eagle Chapter of the Order of the Eastern Star. (ECHS.)

The first gold rush to Fulford, a mining camp located 13 miles southeast of Eagle on Nolan Creek (a tributary to East Brush Creek), started in about 1887. (Fulford is accessed by a 22-mile-long road.) William Nolan was the prospector to strike gold in what became the Fulford Mining District on New York Mountain. By 1892, the district, which encompassed 6 miles, was gaining a reputation as a producer of gold. Miners were also finding copper and indications of silver and lead. More than 500 claims were staked on the mountain. At its peak (around 1900), there were reportedly 600 people living in the mountains around Fulford, and 200 men working in the mines. However, the Panic of 1893 (an economic depression, partially caused by an oversupply of silver) put Fulford on a path of decline. The town was officially platted in 1895, and at the time boasted 25 buildings including two general stores, two hotels, and three saloons, with a population of 100 people. By 1903, only a few determined miners were left in the camp. (ECHS.)

Arthur Fulford

Given by Jackie Gamble

Fulford is named for Arthur Fulford, an adventurer who died tragically on New Year's Eve, 1891. Fulford was well known throughout the valley, having served as Red Cliff town marshall in the early 1880s. By 1891, Fulford had moved down valley. His parents, Edward and Sarah Jane, operated the "Halfway House" stage stop (located between Eagle and Fulford). Legend has it that one day Arthur Fulford was at the Halfway House when a prospector stopped by, claiming to be in possession of a notebook describing the location of a fabulously rich gold mine in the area. According to a story that had circulated for several decades, an avalanche buried the mine and the men working in it in the 1850s. Fulford was initially skeptical, but the stranger had a bag of ore samples to back up his tale. A short time later, the prospector was killed in a bar fight. Fulford found the man's cabin and notes, and set out on New Year's Eve, 1891, to "jump" the claim. However, Fulford got caught in an avalanche and perished on the mountain. He is buried in Red Cliff. (ECHS.)

This photograph shows the remains of a stamp mill (a machine that uses metal "stamps" to crush ore) located above Upper Fulford, on the Doctor Jackpot mining claim. Fulford's second boom started in 1913, when one of the persistent miners who had stayed on made a lucky strike. Once again, the local newspapers were dominated by stories of mining activity in Fulford. One mine, the "1913 Tunnel," reportedly produced ore of a $200-per-ton quality. Miners hurried to the camp and filled the hotels, but the boom and the vein of ore lasted only for a period of weeks. Although some miners were able to extract some quality ore from Fulford, the camp was never successful enough to figure prominently in Colorado history. These days, the town is a summer cabin community of several dozen homes. Some original structures remain in the town, but most are badly deteriorated. (Kathy Heicher.)

Edward and Sarah Jane Fulford claimed their homestead just below the forks of Brush Creek and built the "Halfway House" stage stop in the 1890s, serving the stages that ran the 22-mile route between Eagle and Fulford. Stagecoaches stopped for an hour, while passengers were served a meal, and horses were swapped for a fresh team. The cost of a one-way stage ride to Fulford was $2 and a round-trip ticket was $3.50. The original Halfway House burned down, but was rebuilt in the 1920s and still stands today at the Sylvan Lake State Park Visitor's Center. Below, several Brush Creek women pose for a photograph in about 1900 at the Halfway House. Sitting are, from left to right, Nettie Peterson, Lilly Peterson (baby), and Elizabeth Halloran. Standing are Sarah Jane Fulford (left) and Adelaide (Fulford) Morgan. The Petersons lived on West Brush Creek, on the homestead just above the creek forks. (ECHS.)

Two men who appear to have hiked up Bellyache Mountain take a look toward the northwest at the growing settlement in this 1902 photograph. Note the increase in the number of houses compared with the 1895 photograph on page 25. The little community on Brush Creek was the last settled community where prospectors headed up to the mining camps of the Fulford District could stop for supplies. The photograph shows the start of some town-like characteristics. Note the Methodist Church with a steeple on the right (on what is now Second and Howard Streets), and the more densely developed downtown area to the left. Cattle ranching was a growing economic force in the valley. Although Eagle was not yet officially a town, the residents of the community were already attempting to move the county seat down the valley from Red Cliff. (ECHS; image edited by Mike Crabtree.)

Three

A TOWN IS BORN
1905–1920

By 1905, Eagle had the feel of a small town. The businesses that originally operated out of tents were now located in buildings made of logs, wood, or bricks. A grid street system was taking shape, with businesses lined along the main business district (Broadway, First Street, and Second Street) along with some handsome homes, and a scattering of ranches spread out along Brush Creek and the Eagle River.

Eagle was the last place where miners could find shelter and supplies before heading up to the mining camp of Fulford, at the base of New York Mountain, some 20 miles distant.

The community included a school, church, and social groups such as the Woodmen of the World fraternal order for men, and literary societies for the ladies. However, Eagle lacked any sort of organized central water system, electric light plant, drainage ditches, sidewalks, trees, and police or fire protection. Given the lack of rules and ordinances, it was not unusual for horses, cattle, and dogs to freely roam the streets. In February 1905, prominent rancher John Love circulated a petition calling for incorporation of Eagle into an official town. Community leaders backed the proposal, arguing that a "foundation for the future" had to be laid if the community was going to attract outside capital and continued growth.

Not surprisingly, the election proved to be controversial—a pattern that remains typical of Eagle politics today. While supporters argued that the town organization and community improvements were necessary for the advancement of the community, detractors warned that taxes could be outrageously high.

The March 25, 1905, vote was favorable, with 62 people voting for incorporation, and 20 voting against. The newspaper called for a new era of "business, harmony, and prosperity."

One month later, the town's first election was held. Storekeeper E. E. Glenn was elected as the first mayor of Eagle, and six trustees were named to the town board: T. J. Dice, H. W. Goodrich, S. M. Playford, Peter Thoberg, A. Lumley, and H. A. Hockett. "With these men the town is assured a safe and conservative administration," declared the *Eagle Valley Enterprise*.

This 1908 photograph offers a view down Second Street, looking east. The brick building on the right (the old town hall), constructed in 1904 by Ed Hughes, was the first brick structure in Eagle. The first tenant was the Eagle Club Saloon. The saloon was sold to brothers Byron and Charles Zartman. In 1918, the building was remodeled into a hospital in order to treat patients during the Spanish flu epidemic. When the epidemic ended in 1919, the building was remodeled again into an auto showroom. In 1930, the "Delphian Society," a women's home study group, recognized a need for a place for ranchers' and farmers' wives to gather when they made periodic visits to town. The society purchased the structure for use as a public gathering place. It was known as the "Community House" for many years. During the 1920s, an addition was constructed on the east side for use as a firehouse. Eventually, the building became the town hall. A small library was located upstairs. (ECHS.)

Teams of horses and wagons meet at the intersection of Broadway and Second Street, sometime between 1910 and 1920. The townspeople appear to be gathered for a special event. The E. E. Glenn Store was one of several general merchandise stores in Eagle. That building still stands today and currently houses a bike shop. (ECHS.)

Broadway has always served as Eagle's main street and central business district. Some of the historic buildings visible in this undated photograph are still in place today. Note the J. W. Hugus Company mercantile store in the two-story brick structure on the right. Later the Lewis brothers operated their mercantile store out of that same building. Wells Fargo bank is currently located in the historic structure. (ECHS.)

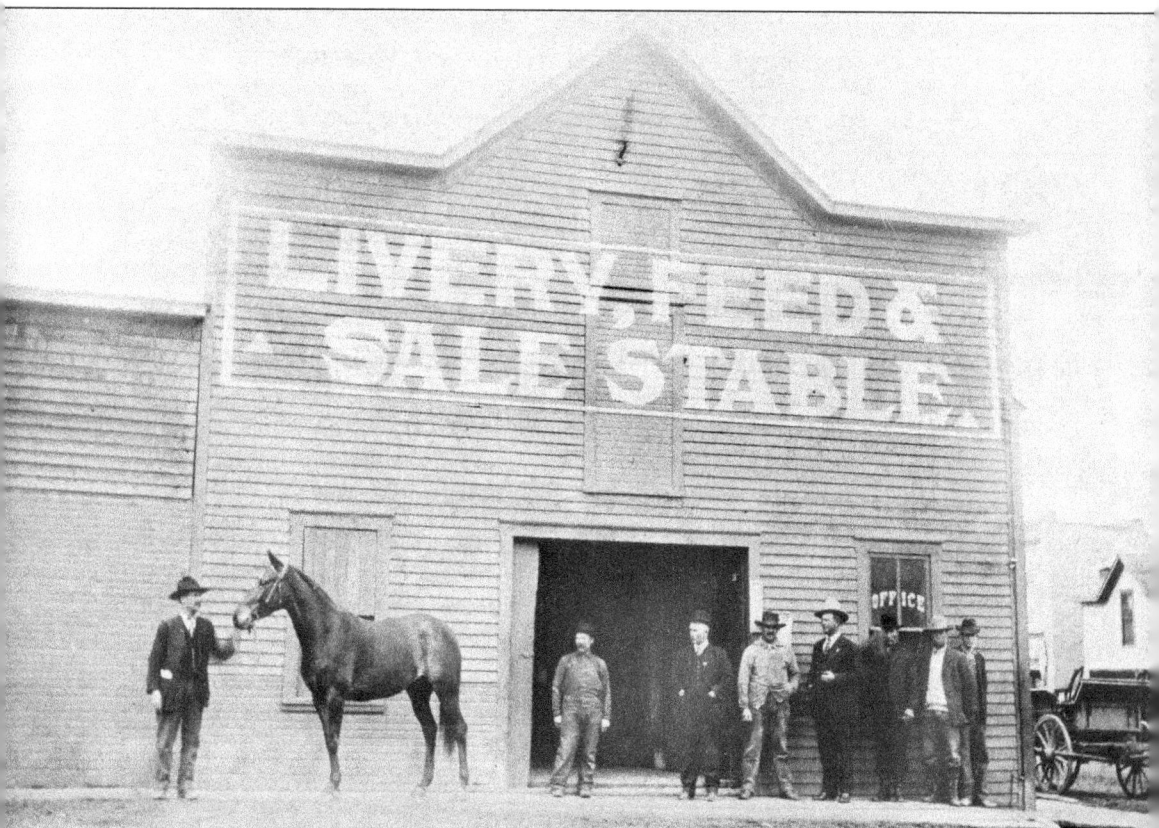

John Buchholz, the second son of Eagle pioneer Nick Buchholz, holds the reins of a horse in this 1908 photograph taken in front of the Buchholz Livery (located on the corner of Second Street and Broadway, where the Eagle Town Hall now stands). Originally built by Marshall and Arthur Fulford in 1889 or 1890, the livery stable was quickly sold to brothers Fred and Ben Hadley, who began the first stage line into the new Fulford mining district. The county had built a road from the Fulford Ranch (near the forks of Brush Creek) to Nolan Creek in 1891 at a cost of $1,000. The Hadley brothers had a government contract to haul mail to Fulford. The Buchholz family acquired the livery and adjacent properties in a land trade. Ranchers and miners could board their horses at the livery when they came to town. The Buchholz family owned the livery stable for 20 years. It was torn down in October 1929. (ECHS.)

Horse races were a popular entertainment and an opportunity for some gambling. The event pictured above took place on April 4, 1908, on what was then called Wood's Lane or Nogal Lane. John Welsh's horse "Rex," ridden by John Buchholz, was matched in a 600-yard sprint against "Grizzly Belle," a horse owned by Jake Borah. Although Grizzly Belle had won a race with Rex the previous summer and was expected to win again, it was Buchholz and Rex (pictured below) who came away with the prize. Regionally, the red-haired, freckle-faced Buchholz was famous for his horse skills, once winning 11 races in a single day. Saddle horses raised and trained by Buchholz were in great demand. (ECHS; photographs edited by Mike Crabtree.)

The community was stunned when Eagle County assessor Nick Buchholz, one of the county's earliest pioneers, died on August 5, 1911. Buchholz, who homesteaded north of Eagle, had served as county assessor for 24 years. The crowd that turned out for his funeral (pictured above) included fellow pioneers, prominent ranchers, businessmen, and county officials. Buchholz's oldest son, Jim, was appointed to fill the vacancy in the assessor position. (ECHS.)

Bill Burt and his horse Kipling stand between freight wagons in what was probably the yard of the Buchholz Livery Stable. This photograph dates to 1908. The Eagle School is visible in the background. (ECHS.)

The Rio Grande Railroad (D&RG)narrow gauge tracks were extended to Eagle in 1887 and were widened to standard gauge in 1891. The railroad's freight-hauling capability was a key factor in Eagle's evolution from a homestead settlement to an organized town. The D&RG built a train depot at Eagle in 1900. (Koonce family collection.)

The first school district in Eagle was established in 1889. Classes were held in various homesteader cabins. In the early 1900s, the townspeople approved a $2,000 bond issue and built this school on land donated by Bill Edwards. In this 1913 photograph, the sixth child from the left in the front row, wearing a hat, is Rolland Randall. The Catholic Church purchased the building in 1915. St. Mary's Catholic Church is located on the site today. (ECHS.)

The United Methodist Church, still located on this site at Second and Howard Streets, was originally built in 1899. Citizens pitched in to help with the labor, but the founding minister, Rev. W. W. Winnie, handled much of the work and most of the expense. The parsonage, at left, was moved in 1958 to the "Randall Heights" neighborhood between Fifth and Sixth Streets on Howard Street. (McCain-Reynolds family collection.)

The "First National Bank of Eagle County" was organized in 1908 and was capitalized at $25,000. The men standing outside the bank are identified as, from left to right, Gull Offerson (a Beaver Creek rancher), Oscar Kempf (developer of the Lady Belle mine), Charles MCarthy, Ben White (Brush Creek rancher), John Welch (Welsh?), Jess Shrock, Bud Tandy, and Art Tandy, one of the original stockholders in the bank. (ECHS; Ping-DeGraw Collection.)

This 1915 photograph shows the stylish Fanny Morgan, a businesswoman who started Eagle's first boutique, the "Serve-U-Shop." The store, located on the west side of Broadway, offered yard goods, accessories, and women's clothing; it also served as a gathering place for local ranch wives and housewives. Morgan's husband, Billy, operated a pool hall next door to the shop. (ECHS.)

The somewhat sketchy information that is available suggests these gentlemen were among the early pioneers of Eagle. Notes accompanying the photograph indicate that among the gentlemen pictured are Metheney (related to the Nogals), Duncan (operator of a hotel), Marquous, Quirk, Wiseman, Jack Stremme, Christ Christensen (a blacksmith), Ben Hadley (stagecoach operator), and McDonald (possibly A. A. McDonald, the man who purchased the town site for back taxes in 1882). (ECHS.)

Tom and Rose Lewis came to Eagle in 1915 to work in the already established Hugus mercantile store. Lewis, with the help of Senator Kluge from Mesa County, bought out Hugus and started the "Lewis-Kluge" country store in the two-story brick building that still stands on the northeast corner of Third Street and Broadway. Pictured are Elizabeth Colleps of Eby Creek, Tom Lewis, and D. M. (Skeet) Kroger. Eventually, Lewis's sons, Harry and John, took over the store operation, then Harry and his wife, Teresa, built it into a well-known general merchandise business that operated until the mid-1970s. Canned goods lined the north wall of the store. There was a cooler and butcher counter in the back corner where Harry cut meat to order. The H. W. Lewis Store was known for its quality cowboy boots and Levi jeans. (ECHS.)

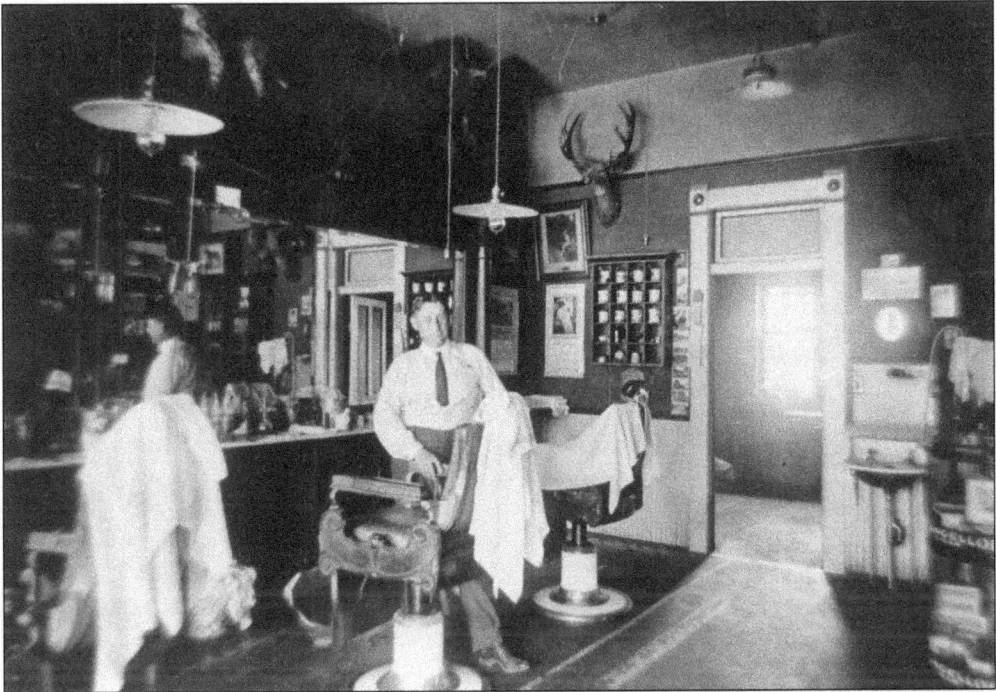

Jack Bindley's "Silver Eagle" barbershop, located in the Dice building, was a modern marvel. The shop featured two leather-upholstered hydraulic barber chairs and wall-sized mirrors. Bindley offered shaves with hot-brush lather and a straightedge razor that he could strop to a fine rhythm. Bindley's son Ira followed him into the business. His daughter Ellen Faye opened a beauty salon in the back of the building. (ECHS.)

From the time the town was officially incorporated in 1905, Eagle community leaders continually pushed for growth and improvements. This photograph, taken sometime after 1913, shows the new, two-story brick school on the right and irrigated pastures in the foreground. (ECHS; Ping-DeGraw Collection.)

Jesse Sherman and his younger brother George purchased their cattle ranch on the Eagle River, about 3 miles east of town, in 1901. For many years, the Sherman brothers were considered outstanding pioneers in the development of potato and grain production in the Eagle River Valley. The Sherman brothers sold their ranch in 1918. George Sherman died a few years later, but Jesse

D. M. "Skeet" Koger, who lived on the Sherman Brothers Ranch, tends a field of Red McClure and Ohio potatoes. Jesse Sherman is holding the irrigation shovel. (ECHS; Laurene Knupp Collection.)

Sherman lived in Eagle until his death in 1953 at the age of 88. What was once the Sherman Brothers Ranch is now the Diamond S Ranch, a large-acre development of mostly second homes. (McCain-Reynolds family collection.)

Jesse Sherman and his wife, Gertrude, often entertained nieces and nephews and children from town. This cement-block home was the primary Sherman residence. Several other houses on the ranch were used for the families that helped to work the ranch. (McCain-Reynolds family collection.)

47

The Eagle Valley had a reputation for raising fine potatoes, but the work could be backbreaking. Harvest began right after the first hard frost nipped the potato vines. Typically, children were pulled out of school to help with harvest. In the photograph above, a harvest crew picks up spuds on a farm near Eagle. Below, field workers on the Sherman ranch use a potato sorter to organize spuds by size. (ECHS; McCain-Reynolds family collection.)

Farm workers in a celebratory mood hoist 100-pound sacks of spuds into a wagon at the Sherman ranch east of Eagle. The next step in the process was for farmers to haul their potatoes to the Denver and Rio Grande Railroad depot at Eagle. From there, they would be shipped to their destination. The railroad photograph dates to 1910. (ECHS; McCain-Reynolds family collection.)

A ranch crew mows hay on the William Mayer Ranch, at the south end of town. This ranch property is now developed into the Mayer Addition, Bull Pasture, and Eagle Ranch subdivisions. The photograph was taken from about where the medical campus now exists, looking east. (ECHS.)

Ranch workers stack hay on the Mayer ranch. The "Mormon Derrick," a horse-powered weight and pulley device, lifted the hay to the top of the stack. Horse teams and rakes "push" hay to the loading area. A couple of antique derricks can still be seen on Brush Creek. (ECHS.)

Ranchers look over the first cutting of hay on July 24, 1914, at the Sherman ranch east of Eagle. Alfalfa and Timothy hay were among the crops that thrived in the mountain valley climate. (McCain-Reynolds family collection.)

A team of horses also provided the muscle for this "slide stacker." The power of the horses allowed ranchers to create huge haystacks. (ECHS.)

A team of three horses pulls a cutter during oat harvest on the Sherman ranch east of Eagle. The soils and climate of the Eagle Valley produced excellent hay and grain crops. This photograph was snapped in the early 1900s. (ECHS.)

The grain binder could cut a wide swath (6 to 8 feet) through a field of ready-to-be harvested grain. As the horses pull the binder forward, the grain stalks are bent inward toward a sickle. The cut grain is then conveyed on a cloth canvas to a gear-driven "knotter" that tied the stalks into a bundle. Field workers would then stack the bundles into teepee-shaped "shocks" for drying. (ECHS.)

Bill and Mattie Randall were married February 4, 1906, in a small house on the corner of Fourth Street and Broadway in Eagle. Witnesses who signed the wedding license were Edna Lemon and Claude Stewart. The Randalls worked a ranch just north of the Eagle River (about where the Interstate 70 interchange is now) and raised four children: Rolland, Harold (Mick), La Veta (Whittaker), and Virginia (Cooper). Pictured below are some members of the extended Randall clan. From left to right are, (first row) Ethel, Rolland, La Veta, Hazel, unknown, and Harold; (second row) Mattie Randall, Minnie, Les Randall, and Myrtie. (Randall family collection/Peggy Buckau.)

Bill Randall was 15 years old when he arrived in Eagle County, via a covered wagon that took him over the Gore Range to McCoy. Among family members, he had the nickname of "Chief." He made his living managing ranches in the Eagle area, including the Woods ranch north of the Eagle River, and he also worked ranches on Brush Creek. He is remembered by his grandchildren for his ready hug and "Grandpa will fix it" attitude, as well as for the crock of homemade sauerkraut that once exploded in the kitchen. Bill was 95 years old when he died in 1975. Pictured below are the Randall children, Rolland, LaVeta, and Mick, in 1913. All of the children spent their lives in Eagle. Rolland worked ranches and was a state patrol dispatcher, LaVeta married rancher Gordon Whittaker, and Mick worked for the Eagle County Road and Bridge Department. (Randall family collection/Peggy Buckau.)

The Eagle School (on the left), built in 1913, was an impressive, two-story, red brick building located on Broadway between Fifth and Sixth Streets. The structure was torn down in the late 1980s due to structural problems. The Eagle County administration building is now located on the site. (ECHS.)

Elementary school students pose in front of the Eagle School in about 1914, when the school first opened. The girl with the long curls in the front row (second from left) is Fannie Gamble, and standing next to her is Imogene Lewis. The first child in the middle row is Nick Buchholz, son of John Buchholz. Third from the left in the top row is Leonard Ping, who grew up to be a photographer. (ECHS.)

By 1913, the people of Eagle recognized a need for a new school building. William Edwards agreed to provide the land if bus service would be provided for the children who lived outside of town. The townspeople and outlying residents agreed to those terms. Initially the upstairs of the building was unfinished and was used as a gym. Below, children pose on the steps of the new Eagle School in 1919. From left to right are, (first row) unidentified, Winona McGinley, John Hartman, Lorraine Essick, John Lewis, Melissa Larsen (Trezise), Leonard Ginther, and unidentified; (second row) Vernice Randall, Charlotte Randall, two unidentified, Bobby Oleson, Viving Heyer, and Florence Johnson; (third row) Eugene Grant, Eugene Essick, Grace Edge, Ethel Cowden, and Howard Brown; (fourth row) unidentified, Harry Lewis, La Veta Randall (Whittaker), Grace McCain, Pauline Reynolds, Gretchen Defoor, and two unidentified; (fifth row) Harold (Mick) Randall, Paddy Sullivan, Burl Cowden, and Donald Ginther. The teacher is Miss E. Lieberman. (Lewis family collection.)

The discovery of silver and copper ore on Horse Mountain (located about 8 miles southeast of Eagle on Salt Creek) in 1912 set off yet another mining boom. Nineteen-year-old George Guenon was tending cattle when he found the ore vein. At the same time, Selma Kempf, the wife of Eagle rancher Oscar Kempf, had a series of dreams of a great silver mine near Eagle. When the Kempfs heard news of Guenon's find, Oscar staked a claim, recruited some business partners, and began exploring what he called the "Lady Belle" mine (named in honor of his wife). The *Rocky Mountain News* ran a front-page story with the headline, "Eagle Strike Real; Prospectors Wild." The men in the photograph are at the entrance to the mine. (Copyright, Colorado Historical Society/Denver and Rio Grande Collection, CHS-X5650.)

THE DISCOVERERS OF THE EAGLE MINING
DISTRICT OF COLORADO. GEORGE GUNNING, WHO FOUND
THE FLOAT (ON THE RIGHT) AND J.O. KEMPF THE LOCATER.

Above, George Guenon (his name is misspelled in the photograph) and Oscar Kempf, credited with being the discoverers of the Eagle Mining District, stand by one of the mining excavations on Horse Mountain. When the news of the mining camp became public on February 12, 1913, dozens of miners began staking claims. The *Eagle Valley Enterprise* predicted that in a two-month period, Eagle was destined to grow from a modest-sized farming town of 500 to a city of 5,000. Rancher Charles Zartman filed a plat for a town he called "Elk Horn" at the base of Horse Mountain. By May 1913, Elk Horn had a population of 100. Below, by the summer of 1913, the settlement near the Lady Belle mine consisted of numerous canvas tents, frame sheds, and a storefront. (Copyright, Colorado Historical Society/Denver and Rio Grande Collection, CHS-X5663 and CHS-X5653.)

Oscar Kempf (sitting in the top row in the center, hands crossed) poses above with the business partners who helped finance the Lady Belle venture. B. B. Yeomans is the man standing in the cut on the mountainside with B. M. White sitting at his feet. Below, men prepare to send off a horse-drawn skid loaded with sacks of ore from the Lady Belle mine. During its height, about 20 tons of ore per day were shipped from the mine. However the vein proved shallow. By 1914, the mining frenzy on Horse Mountain was practically at a standstill. The Lady Belle continued to be worked until about 1918, realizing a total profit of about $450,000. There was some limited prospecting on Horse Mountain in the 1950s and 1960s by prospectors seeking uranium and vanadium. (Copyright, Colorado Historical Society/Denver and Rio Grande Collection, CHS-X5662 and CHS-X5652.)

Sports are the lifeblood of a small town. Baseball was a particularly beloved sport. Every town in the valley had a team and loyal fans. This team played the Denver Bears in a match in 1914. The Bears actually traveled to Eagle, reportedly because they were attempting to recruit the pitcher, Bill Nimon. The game was tied at 5-5 until the last inning, when the local boys lost 7-5. From left to right are, (front row) Eddie Place (catcher) and Bill Nimon (pitcher); (second row) Leo Carey, an unidentified player from Minturn, Roy Dodson, and Frank Stapp; (third row) Lloyd Carey, Omar Howland, Roy Langford, and Charley (Heimie) Hemberger. At left, Omar Howland strikes a pose. (ECHS.)

This westward view of Eagle shows the railroad bridge over the Eagle River. The buildings grouped just beyond the bridge are the Eagle depot and section houses, along with the water tank used to fill steam engines. (ECHS; Ping-DeGraw Collection.)

This studio portrait shows Barbara Gleason (Pearch) who grew up in Eagle. As a young woman, Barbara worked selling movie tickets at the Eagle Theater. Barbara married Tom Pearch of Squaw Creek, who was known locally for his skills as an auctioneer. (Ping-DeGraw collection.)

1930 Town of Eagle

In 1909, the *Eagle Valley Enterprise* declared that Eagle was destined to become the "metropolis of Eagle County" and urged residents to support the construction of a waterworks system. The newspaper editor voiced concern that by lacking a central water system, the town was little more than a "raw frontier village" that was absolutely without defense should a fire break out. The townspeople did support construction of a new system. A promotional brochure produced in 1912 declared, "Eagle has a town site as level as a floor, and well kept streets with a beautiful system of shade trees bordering good walks." The brochure also bragged of the town's $26,000 gravity-fed water system, a three-block park in the center of town, and system of electric lights. (ECHS)

Four

THE NEW COUNTY SEAT
1921–1930

Not a drop of blood was shed in the battle for the Eagle County seat. However, the tug-of-war between the mining town of Red Cliff (Vail's neighbor to the southwest) and the ranching community of Eagle was fierce. The fight went on for 26 years, four spirited elections, and several expensive court battles.

Red Cliff, a raucous mining camp up-valley, was the first organized town in the county. When the state legislature carved out Eagle County in 1883, Red Cliff was the logical choice for county seat. The pioneers of Eagle disagreed and began lobbying for county seat status 10 years before the town was incorporated.

The argument, repeated for the next couple of decades, was that Red Cliff was not centrally located in the county, posing a burden to citizens who had to travel to the county seat to conduct business.

The issue first went to election in 1895. County voters were asked if the county seat should be removed, and if so, to where. Some 303 votes were cast for Eagle, and 197 for Red Cliff. Eagle declared itself the winner. Red Cliff immediately filed a lawsuit challenging the fact that only resident taxpayers were allowed to vote. The Colorado Supreme Court ruled in Red Cliff's favor, and declared that removal of the county seat required a two-thirds majority vote.

The next election, equally fierce, took place in 1904. Insults and accusations flew. Inflammatory rhetoric filled the rival newspapers. Eagle came up short of votes, but not of determination. Eagle won the next election in 1912. Red Cliff sued, and again the court sided with the mining camp.

The deciding vote in 1920 involved some collusion. Eagle leaders promised to support construction of a county high school in neighboring Gypsum, if Gypsum voters would support the county seat move. The strategy worked. On November 11, 1921, the sheriff and three deputies packed up the courthouse records in Red Cliff and loaded them onto a couple of freight cars on a train headed for Eagle.

Thus began a new era of prosperity for the down-valley ranching town.

Agriculture continued to be the driving economic force in the valley in the 1920s. Note the wide-open fields around the edges of town and up the Brush Creek drainage. In the photograph below, the tall building on the left is the Woodman Hall (located where the Brush Creek Saloon now stands). Constructed in 1898, the open upstairs space was used as a meeting place for the Woodmen of the World fraternal organization. The upstairs space was also used for dances, movies, programs, and sports (at one time, high school basketball was played at the Woodman Hall). The lower floor saw a variety of uses, including store space. When Eagle won the county seat fight in 1921, the county administrative offices were initially housed in this building. The original structure was demolished in 2007. (ECHS; Ping-DeGraw Collection.)

A mounted eagle and elk greeted visitors to the First National Bank of Eagle County. Pictured are teller Erwin Cramp (left) and bank president Joseph D. Allen. Allen started his banking career as a teller at the bank in Red Cliff. After the county seat was moved to Eagle in 1921, Allen and his wife, Helen (Hart), moved to Eagle, where they were active in the community for many decades. Joe Allen had a reputation as a compassionate banker. He served as a director of the Federal Reserve Bank of Kansas City. One of the Allen daughters, Jean Johnson, was instrumental in forming the Eagle County Historical Society and helped to develop the archive collection. The photograph below offers a glimpse of the inside of the teller's cage at the bank. (ECHS.)

Otis and Minnie Ping bought the Nogal Hotel in 1923. The Pings expanded the commercial operation by adding two wings out back and several detached motel units. Minnie Ping was an ambitious businesswoman, and Otis was the handyman who did the work. The Pings eventually installed a gas station, featuring a glass-bubble pump. Their son Leonard operated a photography lab in the building. Leonard and his sister Garnett lived on the property for most of their lives. Family members recently found hundreds of photographs in the building. This is the same structure pictured on the cover of this book. (ECHS; Ping-DeGraw Collection.)

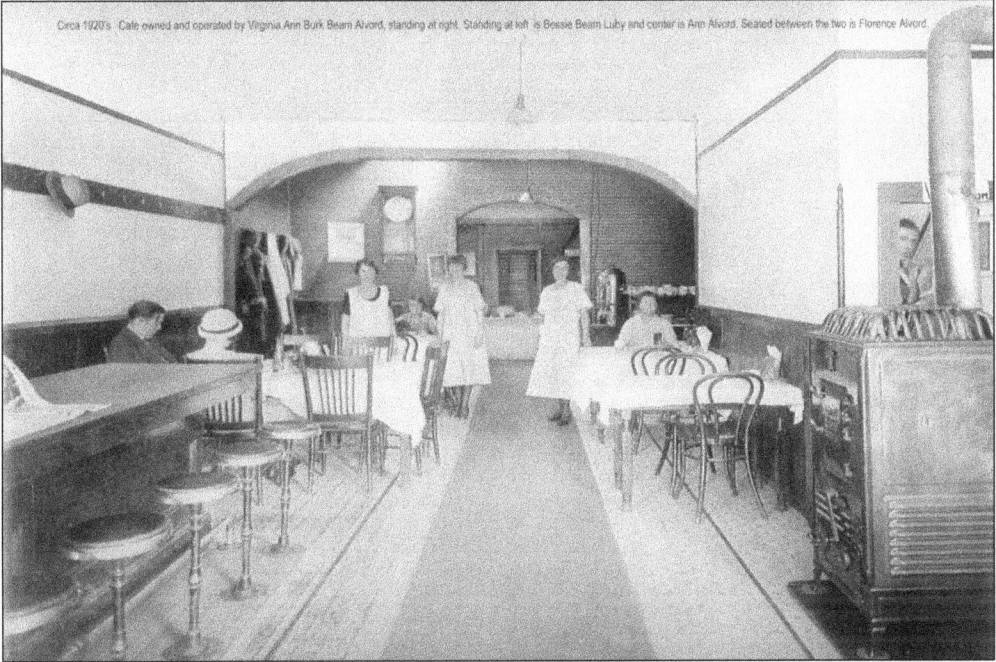

Virginia Ann Burk Beam Alvord operated the Alvord Café on the east side of Broadway in the 1920s. The kitchen was in the rear, with a half dozen tables up front. Alvord and her daughters lived upstairs. Standing left is Bessie Beam Luby (wife of Judge Bill Luby), standing center is Ann Alvord, and seated between the two ladies is Florence Alvord. (ECHS.)

Elephants were most certainly not a common sight in Eagle. The owners of this lumber and hardware company found a unique way to advertise their business. The pachyderm appears to be walking down Broadway. Note the cement-block house in the background. (ECHS; Ping-DeGraw Collection.)

The Ku Klux Klan made an appearance in Eagle in the mid-1920s at the same time the organization was becoming politically powerful throughout the state. On an evening in April 1926, Klan members burned a cross and set off an explosion near the Christensen ranch in the west part of town. Catholics were often the targets of their harassment. An attempt by the Klan to elect a slate of town board candidates that year was rejected by voters in a record turnout. (ECHS; Ping-DeGraw Collection.)

Louis Couquoz and Ernie Nogal (the son of pioneer Charley Nogal) pose in front of an automobile filled with mule deer. Couquoz was considered to be something of a mountain man. For a time, he homesteaded at Joe Good meadow on East Brush Creek. Nogal did some commercial hunting for the mining camps. (ECHS.)

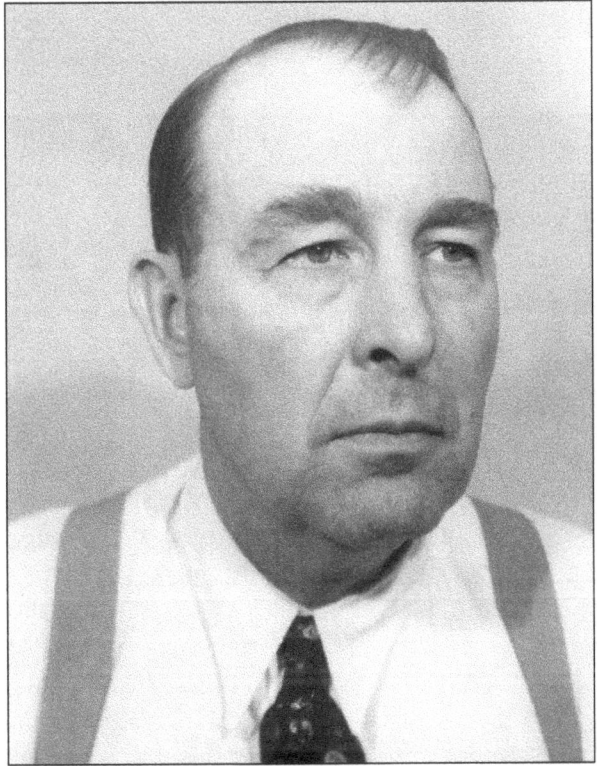

Murray Wilson was appointed to the job of Eagle County sheriff in 1922 and remained in that position for 37 years. A self-trained law officer, Wilson handled cases that ranged from bootlegging, to railroad strikes, to murder. Wilson had a reputation as a compassionate and understanding lawman. He rarely had need for a gun. He earned the respect of the people he arrested, as well as those who never had a brush with the law. A modest man, he declined when the *Saturday Evening Post* magazine requested an interview. Below, Murray enjoys an outing with his wife Alberta, daughter-in-law Thelma, and grandchildren Willard and Shirley (Shelton). (ECHS; and Wilson family collection.)

Every town loves a parade. In 1922, community leaders decided the time was right for an annual celebration. The upcoming event was announced in the newspaper, and residents were asked to suggest a name. Minnie Nimon submitted the winning entry of "Eagle's Annual Flight," and the first "Flight Days" parade was held Saturday, September 22, 1922. The celebration featured a speech on the challenges facing farmers by Professor Gillette of the Colorado State Agricultural College. Some 1,500 people turned out for a free barbecue beef lunch followed by a baseball game between the Eagle and Edwards teams. (Eagle lost, 17-14.) The afternoon schedule featured a "flivver (car) relay race" and a horse race. The celebration ended in the evening with a dance at the Woodman Hall. Over the years, Flight Days has developed into a three-day celebration, staged the fourth weekend in June. (ECHS; Ping-DeGraw Collection.)

Teacher E. W. Jerrell taught all 30 Eagle High School students in 1923. In the first row are, from left to right, Nick Buchholz, Dwight Carlson, Fannie Gamble, Nellie Sullivan, Bessie Beam, Charlotte Hart, Winona Reynolds, and Clarence "Cob" Rule; (second row) Leonard Ping, "Butsie" Gamble, Floyd Ping, Ocie Hart, Irene Baker, Josephine Schrupp, Morton White, Lloyal Carlson, Gideon Ruggles, and Myron McGinley; (third row) Ruby Ping, Vinta Byers, Marjorie Jerrell, unidentified, Alice Hart, Mary Baker, Florence Alvord, Imogene Lewis, and Barcus Butler; (fourth row) Lewis Cowden, Charles Byers, and Rolland Randall. (Lewis family collection.)

Mary Frances "Fanny" Gamble and her mother, Mary Hannah (Buchholz) Johnston, prepare for an outing. Gamble graduated from Eagle High School in 1923. She taught school at Dotsero and on the Piney and worked as a bookkeeper for many years at the First National Bank and Koonce Chevrolet. (ECHS; Ping-DeGraw Collection.)

Howard McCain poses outside the Eagle High School with his 1923 Chevy hot rod. Howard grew up on the Sherman ranch. He and his wife, Marilla, became publishers of the *Eagle Valley Enterprise* weekly newspaper. (McCain-Reynolds family collection.)

Siblings Harry and Imogene Lewis mug for the camera outside of their home in Eagle. Harry operated the H. W. Lewis mercantile store in Eagle for many years. In their youth, he and his brother John were among the town's best baseball players. (Lewis family collection.)

Small towns love their high school sports, and basketball was big in Eagle. Because the school lacked a gym until 1940, home games were played in the Woodman Hall downtown. Players had to work around such obstacles as a heating stove and pillars. Potato-sorter screens were used to protect windows. Pictured are the Eagle High School boys and girls basketball teams of the 1924–1925 season. At right, Rolland Randall poses in his EHS uniform in 1925. (Lewis and Randall family collections.)

Leonard Ping grew up in Eagle and graduated from Eagle High School in 1923. For many years he ran a photography business out of the Ping Hotel. Using his camera, Leonard captured life in Eagle from the 1920s through the 1940s, taking formal studio portraits as well as landscape photographs and shots of everyday life in Eagle. Leonard snapped many of the photographs in this book. Below, a family poses for a portrait in what appears to be the backyard "studio" of the Ping residence. Leonard and his sister Garnett lived at the Ping complex all of their lives. (ECHS; Ping-DeGraw Collection.)

Despite the small size of the student population, the Eagle High School always had an orchestra. This is the ECHS orchestra of 1925–1926. Pictured are, from left to right, Barcus Butler (drums), Robert Pemberton, Ethel Cowden, Burl Cowden, Eldon Wilson, and unknown. (Lewis family collection.)

The Eagle High School offered a surprising number of athletic opportunities, including basketball for both boys and girls. Pictured above is the tennis club of 1928. From left to right are (first row) Helen Jerrell Dempewolf, Pauline Reynolds Beyers, LaVeta Randall Whittaker, Grace Edge Eaton, Amy Jerrell, and Marillia Reynolds McCain; (second row) Nell Pontius (teacher), Harry White, Don McCauley, John Lewis, Harold (Mick) Randall, and Jeanette Kiley Buchholz (teacher); (third row) John Hartman, Allen Redmond, Harry Lewis, Willie Johnston, Franklin Krebs, and Robert Brown. School Superintendent E. W. Jerrell stands at the top. The town had a dirt-surface tennis court. (ECHS; Laurene Knupp collection.)

An eccentric English cattle rancher named Anthony Sneve was the first settler at the head of West Brush Creek (now Sylvan Lake State Park) in about 1911. Sneve, reportedly hurt by a failed romance, disliked females of any kind, animal or human, and would not tolerate their presence on his property. He was also fiercely protective of the prime trout stream that meandered across his ranch. In 1935, the aging Sneve sold his homestead (pictured above) to William Johnson and moved to Denver. Johnson in turn sold the property to Otto Zurcher in 1943. Zurcher wanted to use the property as a mink farm (note the structures in the photograph below). He also dammed Sneve's hay meadow to create a lake, intending to build cabins and run a fishing resort. Zurcher's dream ended in 1956, when a fire destroyed several key buildings. In 1961, the Colorado Game and Fish Department purchased the property in a foreclosure sale. In 1989, Colorado State Parks acquired the property. (Bill Johnson collection.)

Despite the work of their everyday lives, Eagle residents enjoyed trips up into the nearby mountains to hunt, fish, hike, or simply enjoy a picnic. Above, a carload of adventurers heads to the hills. Below, the Lewis and Cave families enjoy a picnic in the aspen. (ECHS; Ping-DeGraw Collection; and Lewis family collection.)

East Brush Creek with its trout streams and beautiful scenery has always been a popular destination and remains so today. During the 1920s, the Eagle Chamber of Commerce promoted the country around town as the "Heart of the Rocky Mountain Wonderland." The locals didn't need to read the promotional materials. They already knew the good fishing and hunting spots. Below, siblings Harry and Imogene Lewis and a few friends head out on a camping trip in 1929. (Lewis family collection.)

Imogene Lewis and friends work at putting up a pole tent at their camp. Below, the girls haul some firewood into camp. Yeoman Park remains one of the most popular campgrounds on East Brush Creek. Colorado State Parks and the Forest Service now own the land on the East and West forks of Brush Creek that was once held by private owners. Now known as "Sylvan Lake State Park," the area is protected from future development and is considered to be a crown jewel of the State Parks system. (Lewis family collection.)

By 1929, cars had replaced horses and wagons as the preferred mode of transportation. The Buchholz Livery was torn down that year, making way for a Texaco gas station at Second Street and Broadway. This view is to the south, toward Hardscrabble Mountain. (ECHS.)

Local veterans march down Eagle's main street in the 1930 Memorial Day parade. Note that the Buchholz Livery is no longer in place. The businesses in the middle of the block (on the east side of Broadway) include a restaurant and the *Eagle Valley Enterprise* offices. (ECHS; Ping-DeGraw Collection.)

Five

WEATHERING THE DEPRESSION
1929–1939

Despite the stock market crash of 1929, Eagle's community leaders were optimistic at the start of the 1930s.

"Our people were not hurt directly. The crash on Wall Street has hardly been noticeable locally," wrote lawyer Hume S. White in a New Year's essay in the *Eagle Valley Enterprise* on January 3, 1930. Banker J. D. Allen noted that the agricultural community was coming off a decade of "satisfactory" prices for farm produce, livestock, and dairy products. Mine operator John Weiskopf reported that the Fulford District was flourishing, citing specifically the Colerick strike, with a vein of gold and silver averaging $54 a ton; and the discovery of manganese at the base of New York Mountain, carrying good values in silver, lead, copper, zinc, and some gold.

The optimistic outlook probably reflected the fact that Eagle had already weathered several boom-and-bust cycles in the mining industry.

Eventually, of course, the Depression did catch up with Eagle. Because it was an agricultural community, people tended not to go hungry in hard times. Everybody had vegetable gardens, and most had chickens, pigs, cows, and of course the ever-abundant game meat. Many lived by the philosophy of a popular little ditty of the time: "Make it do, wear it out, fix it up, or do without." The women of the Eagle Garden Club prepared Christmas baskets and gifts for needy families.

Still, there were good times. A grand new brick county courthouse was built at the south end of Broadway. A new gym was added to the high school in 1939.

Prohibition ended in 1933, making way for saloons and ending the need for surreptitious alcohol imbibing that had characterized the 1920s. Community dances were staged frequently. Boxing matches were a draw at Wayne Jones's Diamond J Ranch, a few miles east of town.

Although the business of growing head lettuce and potatoes was not quite as prosperous as it had been in the 1920s, agriculture continued as the driving economic force. Sheep were introduced into the valley, touching off a battle between cattlemen and the sheep ranchers that continued for years.

Along with the move of the county seat came an obligation to build a modern county courthouse. Designed by renowned architect J. Francis Pillsbury, the Eagle County Courthouse was constructed in 1932 at a cost of $60,000. The sheriff's office was on the basement floor along with living quarters for the jailer. The jail and courtroom were on the third floor (note the bars on the window at left). (ECHS; Ping-DeGraw Collection.)

The Denver and Rio Grande Railroad depot was operated around the clock. Two water towers allowed steam engines to take on water between Grand Junction and Pueblo. The railroad also provided section houses for workers. (ECHS; Ping-DeGraw Collection.)

Bert Wolverton and Art Koonce were partners in this ranch located immediately north of Eagle in the vicinity of what is now the Interstate 70 interchange. The ranch was eventually sold to Ross Chambers. This view is looking east with Red Point in the background. The barn in the photograph has since been moved to Chambers Park in Eagle, where it serves as the Eagle County Historical Society Museum. The interstate highway now runs through what would have been the middle of the ranch. (Koonce family collection.)

Ranchers often drove their cattle through town while moving them from summer to winter range, a practice that continued well into the 1980s. The drives usually took place in the early morning. There always seemed to be a few errant animals that would make a run through local flower gardens and yards, much to the chagrin of the town's housewives. (ECHS; Ping-DeGraw Collection.)

Although the cattlemen, as the first established ranchers in the area, initially resisted the introduction of sheep, eventually the U.S. Forest Service set up rules that allowed the competing operations to coexist. Above, a flock of sheep roams through the Ping property in Eagle. (ECHS; Ping-DeGraw Collection.)

Fred and Helen Dice came to Brush Creek to ranch in 1931 and stayed through the mid-1940s. They ranched a couple different properties on the creek, in between the Frost Creek and Beecher Gulch drainages. Helen Dice wrote about both the hard work and the pleasures of ranching during those Depression years in her book *A Cup of Clear Cold Water: Life on Brush Creek*. Above, Joe Dice, who was just two years old when his parents came to Eagle, stands beside a potato digger driven by Frank Schoonover. They are harvesting potatoes on the Shrack place (in the vicinity of what is now the Mosher subdivision) on lower Brush Creek. Below, 100-pound sacks of potatoes are loaded onto a wagon. The potatoes would then be taken to spud cellars to be sorted and stored until they were shipped to market. (ECHS; Dice Family Collection.)

The *Eagle Valley Enterprise*, a weekly newspaper, has published continually in Eagle since May 24, 1901. Adrian Reynolds Jr., a Kansas newspaperman, ardent Republican, and community activist, purchased the *Enterprise* in 1918. The Reynolds family published the newspaper for 54 years. A devastating fire on January 13, 1932, destroyed the newspaper office on Broadway. The fire started in an adjacent dry-cleaning shop and wiped out several main street businesses. George Carlow sounded the fire alarm, but the town's limited fire equipment malfunctioned in the freezing temperatures. The building was a complete loss. The only items rescued were a linotype machine (under a blanket in the street), a few cases of type, the forms for that week's newspaper, and a subscription list. Still, Reynolds never missed a week of publication. For the next year, the newspaper was printed in Glenwood Springs, while a new office was built for the *Enterprise*. (ECHS; Ping-DeGraw Collections; McCain-Reynolds family collection.)

When Ade Reynolds died in 1949, his daughter Marilla McCain and her husband, Howard, took over as publishers of the newspaper. A spunky redhead, Marilla was the writer, editor, and proofreader. Howard handled the mechanics of the printing press. Like her father, Marilla was a staunch Republican and a community activist. Her to-the-point writing style and wicked sense of humor, often related in her popular "Around Town" column, made her one of the most widely quoted journalists on Colorado's Western Slope. Marilla played a key role in the building of the original Eagle Valley Medical Center and fought to protect West Slope water resources. The hardworking editor died in 1972 at the age of 58. The paper is now part of the Colorado Mountain News Media holdings. Marilla and Howard, pictured below, enjoy a family picnic on Brush Creek. (McCain-Reynolds family collection.)

This photograph of Broadway, snapped in about 1935, shows Cramp's Grocery on the right. Note the "Highway 40" (what is now Highway 6) sign in the middle of the street. Although the town's streets at this point were still unpaved, they were graded and surfaced with river gravel. (ECHS.)

The Upper Brush Creek School (also called the "Fulford School") was constructed in 1916, just above the fork of East and West Brush Creeks, serving Fulford and the ranch families along the creek. This building, which still stands on West Brush Creek, was last used in 1941, when the school districts were consolidated. Teacher Mary Bemis poses with an unidentified girl. (ECHS.)

Chicago businessman Clyde Lloyd purchased the Sherman Brothers Ranch (east of town) in 1922. He and his stepson Wayne T. Jones called the operation "Red Mountain Ranch" and were known for annually hosting one of the largest Hereford sales in the state. Clyde's brother and sister-in-law, Carl and Ella, were the caretakers for the ranch. Located about 4 miles east of Eagle, the property featured a magnificent ranch house (which burned to the ground in October 1936) and numerous outbuildings, several of which are still in place today. The ranch had ample space for raising cattle and growing hay. Below, cowboys work steers in a corral at the ranch. The ranch brand was a "Diamond J Bar." The property is currently the site of the Diamond Star subdivision. (John Oleson collection.)

The Lloyd brothers pose with fellow cowboys at Red Mountain Ranch. Carl Lloyd Jr. (son of Carl) is third from left, and Clyde (C. F.) Lloyd is third from right. There was also a third Lloyd brother, Frank. The cowboy pictured below is Hershey Wilson, who worked for the Lloyds and somehow earned the nickname of "The Danville Sharpshooter." Wilson was perhaps best known for his boxing skills. Boxing matches, called "smokers," were popular in the 1930s. Wayne T. Jones, stepson of Clyde Lloyd, organized the boxing matches, staged in a stable at the ranch. While some of the locally recruited boxers did not fare so well (one ended up on his rear end in a bucket of water), Wilson attained recognition as Colorado's lightweight champion. (John Oleson collection.)

The Lloyd house was considered one of the most beautiful ranch homes on the Western Slope and was something of a showplace. Ella Lloyd was hosting a party of ladies at a bridge luncheon in October 1936 when a fire was discovered in the attic. When the fire alarm was sounded, about half the men in town showed up to fight the fire. Because the inner walls of the building were made of cement block, the fire burned slowly, and the men and women were able to carry out much of the furniture. However, the ranch water system proved too small to effectively fight the fire, and the building was destroyed. Many of the bystanders wept as the home burned. The loss of the house was estimated at $45,000, along with $7,000 in lost furnishings. (John Oleson collection.)

Clyde (C. F.) Lloyd and his wife Adele, owners of the Red Mountain Ranch, were Chicago residents who spent their summers in Eagle. Late in the 1920s, Lloyd obtained a special-use permit from the Forest Service that allowed him to develop a mountain camp at Lake Charles, a high-country lake on East Brush Creek. Lloyd and other family members built half a dozen cabins, including a cook's cabin and a "honeymoon" cabin on unpatented mining claims at the site. Adele named the resort "Skyland in the Rockies." The Lloyds produced postcards (pictured above) to promote the resort. Mystic Island Lake, pictured on the card, is located about a mile beyond Lake Charles. (During their tenure, the Lloyds renamed the lake "Lake Adele.") The mountain beyond the lake is Eagle Peak. (ECHS and John Oleson collection.)

Carl and Christine (Oleson) Lloyd pose on a dock at the Skyland resort at Lake Charles in the 1930s. Guests accessed the 11,300-foot-high "Skyland" camp by driving to the end of East Brush Creek Road and riding horses up the approximate 6-mile trail that started where the road ended on East Brush Creek (now the Fulford Cave campground). Upon reaching the camp, visitors would be welcomed with coffee, lemonade, and hot doughnuts. The cook and the wranglers pampered guests. In addition to incredible high-mountain scenery, both Lake Charles and Mystic Island Lake offered some great fishing for cutthroat trout. They remain popular destinations for backpackers and hikers. By the late 1940s, the cabins, weathered by high-mountain snows, had fallen into disrepair. The Forest Service dismantled the remaining buildings. (John Oleson collection.)

William Sears Brown served as the Eagle District Ranger for the U.S. Forest Service from 1920 through 1935. Ranger Brown and his family built a ranger station and a cabin at Yeoman Park, 17 miles east of Eagle on East Brush Creek. The ranger station, pictured above, served as the local Forest Service headquarters, where Brown took care of business such as clearing trails, issuing hunting licenses, and managing livestock grazing allotments. Charles Peak is the high mountain in the background. Brown was the driving force behind the construction of the road from Eagle to Thomasville. He also explored the possibility of developing Fulford Cave (on East Brush Creek) into a tourist attraction that would be marketed as "a wonder of the Rocky Mountain Region." There was also talk of damming East Brush Creek at Yeoman Park. Neither of those projects was realized. (Bill Johnson collection.)

The Browns raised their five sons in the Forest Service cabin at Yeoman Park during summer months. When school was in session, Myrtle Brown and the children lived in Boulder, while Bill Brown stayed at a house in Eagle. As soon as school was out for the summer, the family hurried back to the mountains they loved. In 1935, Ranger Brown was promoted to the position of building supervisor for the White River and Holy Cross National Forests. A master finish carpenter by trade, he was instrumental in the construction of new Forest Service offices and houses throughout the region. Brown supervised the crew that constructed this Forest Service office and house in Eagle in 1937, as well as similar facilities at Minturn, Glenwood Springs, and Basalt. Brown retired from the Forest Service in 1944. (Bill Johnson collection.)

The U.S. Forest Service managed timber sales. Trees to be harvested were identified, appraised, and then sold to the highest bidder. Some 25 percent of the revenues went to Eagle County. Information accompanying this photograph indicates the logging was done in the Derby country, north of Eagle. The driver is identified as "Budsey." (ECHS; Ping-DeGraw Collection.)

Although Prohibition became law in Colorado in 1916, it never really stopped determined people from finding a drink. Still, when the liquor ban was lifted nationwide in 1933, bars made a comeback. This saloon was undoubtedly in Eagle, but the photograph did not offer details about where or the identity of the bartender. (ECHS; Ping-DeGraw Collection.)

Art Koonce (pictured below) was 21 years old when he arrived in Eagle in 1901. He worked at a sawmill and did some ranching. However, he had always been fascinated with engines. That interest prompted him to venture in the garage business. He built the first concrete-floored, sheet metal–clad garage building in town at 388 Washington Street and sold Willys-Overland cars. In 1928, Koonce built his second garage on Broadway (currently the location of Red Canyon High School). Koonce Chevrolet was a prominent business downtown for the next 30 years. Always civic-minded, Koonce served several terms as Eagle mayor. He was instrumental in replacing the town's original wooden water pipes with cast iron pipe. Koonce was also a founder of the "Eagle Commercial Club," which became the Chamber of Commerce. (Koonce family collection.)

In 1938, Art Koonce added a modern Phillips 66 service station to his business holdings. The station was located on Highway 6, directly behind the Koonce Chevrolet building (where the orange metal structure is now located). Pictured below are some of the employees who worked for the Koonce businesses. The people sitting on the bench are unidentified. Standing in the doorway are Leo Neumann and Foster Smith. Note the service station attendants' hats. The Koonces operated the Chevrolet agency for 30 years (giving up the franchise in 1963) and held a distributorship with the Phillips Petroleum Company for 40 years. (Koonce family collection.)

Art Koonce poses with his son Harold. After obtaining a college degree and serving a stint in the navy, Harold returned to the family business. When competition from large car dealers made the small operation in Eagle impractical, Harold closed the car dealership and started a new business. His venture, Hometown Supply, provided paper products to businesses in the growing community of Vail. Like his father, Harold was active in the community, serving terms on the town board and taking a leadership role on the Chamber of Commerce. He was instrumental in bringing an airfield to Cooley Mesa and in bringing Colorado Mountain College to the valley. In his retirement years, Harold penned a couple of manuscripts documenting Eagle history. Below, new 1941 Chevys are displayed on Broadway in front of the Koonce building. Note that the gas pumps are gone from the sidewalk, but the main street is still unpaved. (Koonce family collection.)

County road and bridge worker George Nimon runs heavy machinery on what appears to be Brush Creek Road. Les Randall was the county's road boss, and his crew included Nimon, Earl Yost, and Mick Randall. During the 1930s, much work was done to improve Brush Creek Road. Contractor C. A. Switzer built the Crooked Creek Pass road over the top of West Brush Creek, connecting Eagle with Frying Pan Valley. Below, little girls are dwarfed by a gravel crusher. (ECHS.)

Ernie Nogal (right) examines a donkey handled by an unidentified man. The original Nogal ranch is now the site of the Red Canyon Town Homes and Eagle Villas housing developments. (Ping-DeGraw family.)

This group of women and their husbands were pioneers of Eagle. From left to right are Cora Mayer, whose husband, William, ran the Mayer Ranch (now the Eagle Ranch subdivision); Rosetta Nogal (wife of Charley); Alice Bacon (a local historian); ? Hockett; and Carolyn Thoberg. Women's organizations such as the Eagle Garden Club were instrumental in community improvement projects. (John Oleson collection.)

Eldon Wilson, the son of Sheriff Murray Wilson, was something of a visionary who was often at the forefront of bringing new technology to Eagle. Wilson sold and serviced radios and created the town's first public address system. Below, Wilson (at right) and a friend set up that system in preparation for a baseball game. Wilson is also credited with bringing television to town in the 1950s. He devised an over-the-air signal relay system that was located on Castle Peak. (Wilson and Koonce family collections.)

Eldon Wilson was probably the first person to visualize the sagebrush flat on Cooley Mesa, halfway between Eagle and Gypsum, as an airplane landing field. Always fascinated with flying, Wilson, together with friends Eddie Belding and Harold "Mick" Randall, borrowed a county maintainer and scraped off a strip of sagebrush to create a runway for their model planes. Above, Belding and Wilson pose with a plane at the airfield in 1939. Belding went on to become a B-25 pilot during World War II. In the mid-1940s, with Wilson leading the charge, Eagle community leaders persuaded the county to acquire the land for a "flying field." In 1947, in a ceremony featuring a speech by Colorado governor Lee Knaus, the field was officially designated an emergency landing strip for the Civil Aeronautics Authority. Today the Eagle County Regional Airport is located on the site. (ECHS.)

By 1939, community leaders decided it was time to call attention to Eagle's agricultural economy with the first ever Eagle County Fair. The big event was staged on the grounds of Eagle High School on September 16. In addition to 4-H kids competing with their projects, there were competitions for established ranchers and their wives. When the judging was done, a free barbecue lunch was served to 1,200 people. Afterwards the crowd watched a football game between the Minturn and Eagle High School teams (Eagle won, 27-0), listened to a concert by the Eagle County High School band, and attended a free movie. A dance in the evening completed the celebration. Although the event was considered a success, the start of World War II had a big impact on local ranchers. The next big fair was held in 1947. (ECHS; photograph edited by Mike Crabtree.)

Eagle County Fair 1939

Young competitors anxiously await word from the judge at the 1939 Eagle County Fair. Judges were brought in from the extension service at the Colorado Agricultural College in Fort Collins. (ECHS; Ping-Degraw Collection; edited by Mike Crabtree.)

Rodeos were a popular entertainment in a community where many people lived on ranches. This 1939 event was staged on the west side of the Eagle County Courthouse, in what is now the town park. (ECHS; edited by Mike Crabtree.)

Despite the financial hardships of the Depression, people found ways to entertain themselves. High school sporting events drew out the entire community, no matter what the season. A gymnasium was added to the south side of the Eagle School in 1940. The most spirited competition was always the games between Eagle High School and its down-valley rival Eagle County High School (in Gypsum). (ECHS; Ping-DeGraw Collection.)

Six

A Time of Change
1940s

The 1940s ushered in an era of long-lasting changes for the Eagle community.

Eagle closed out the 1930s by hosting the first ever County Fair on the Eagle School grounds at Sixth Street and Broadway. Over 1,200 people turned out to celebrate the county's agricultural success. Nervous 4-H children presented their livestock and projects to the judges. Adult ranchers and their wives competed with exhibitions of crops, stock, and canned vegetables. Eagle was a ranching community and proud of it.

World War II changed everything. Instead of reports about the local potato crops and ranching issues, the front page of the *Eagle Valley Enterprise* offered stories about the young men who had been called to war. "We are furnishing the most healthy, robust men of the entire country for the service," declared Charles S. Merrill, secretary of the local Selective Service Board. The resulting labor shortage hampered production on local ranches.

Patriotic townspeople joined the American Legion, Red Cross, and civil defense organizations. They raised money at war bond rallies. The ladies of the Eagle Garden Club collected salvage items for the war effort including copper, brass, rags, and silk and nylon hosiery. Groups of the local young women (chaperoned, of course), traveled up-valley to dance with the soldiers of the 10th Mountain Division's Camp Hale training facility.

After the war, the economic trends changed. New transportation, shipping, and production methods made it hard for small-scale Eagle ranchers to compete nationally. The returning soldiers had new interests other than ranching.

The December 31, 1948, issue of the *Enterprise* acknowledged that the local agricultural community was now sharing its "top industry" status with other businesses, including lumber production and mining. The newspaper also noted "recreation has come to the front in various parts of the county."

That statement proved somewhat prophetic. By the early 1960s, some of those soldiers who wintered at Camp Hale returned to develop the Vail ski resort, 30 miles up-valley from Eagle. The start of that recreation industry was also the end of Eagle's early era. The next 50 years are an entirely different story.

By the mid-1940s, Eagle's main street had finally been paved by the Colorado Highway Department. The women of the local Home Demonstration Club took on the task of painting a yellow stripe down the middle, using paint left over from somebody's kitchen walls. Eagle was a popular destination for hunters, fishermen, and campers, and had several motels and cottage businesses to tend to their needs. (ECHS; Ping-DeGraw Collection; Koonce family collection.)

The Eagle Theater, located on the west side of Broadway, was the source of entertainment for most of the community. John Greve and his son Lloyd remodeled the old Woodman Hall into a theater, adding a sloping floor and fixed seating. Because the theater had a stage, it was frequently used for town meetings and political gatherings. (ECHS; Ping-DeGraw Collection.)

By the 1940s, the *Eagle Valley Enterprise* had moved into new digs at 333 Broadway. The newspaper office was in the front, and the printing press was in the back. *Enterprise* editor Marilla McCain, center, poses with Lyle Lupton and a friend. (McCain-Reynolds collection.)

After a 1933 fire destroyed several downtown buildings, the next business to build in that space was the Independent Lumber Company. The lumber company moved to Chambers Avenue (across the Eagle River) in the early 1980s. The Eagle Town Hall is now located on the corner where this building once stood. (ECHS; Ping-DeGraw Collection.)

Gas stations were full-service in those days, with uniformed attendants who offered to check oil, wash windshields, and pump gas. This Conoco station was located on Highway 6. (ECHS; Ping-DeGraw Collection.)

Eagle dealt with its share of deep snow. Mim Sharpe, mother of George Carlow, poses outside of Sharpe's Pool Hall and Liquor Store. The pool hall was a popular stopping-off point for men who wanted to grab a hamburger or a beer and perhaps get in a quick card game. Stanley's Cash Grocery, next door, was one of several small grocery stores in town. (ECHS; Ping-DeGraw Collection.)

The ladies of the Eagle Garden Club were usually the driving force behind the Christmas decorations in town. Christmas trees and garlands decked downtown Broadway intersections. Occasionally some driver who had been enjoying some Christmas libations would collide with the tree. (ECHS; Ping-DeGraw Collection.)

Pres. Franklin Roosevelt's economic recovery program during the Great Depression came to Eagle in 1940 with the establishment of a Civilian Conservation Corps (CCC) camp at Yeoman Park. A camp that had previously been located at Meredith (on the Frying Pan drainage) was disassembled and moved to East Brush Creek. About 250 CCC workers reported. One of their primary projects was to improve Brush Creek Road above the forks. Ranchers and Forest Service employees gathered for a "fire warden" meeting at the park in August 1940. Among the men in the picture are, from left to right, (first row) Clyde Schlegel, Cyrus Dice, Forest Ranger Ben Rice, LeRoy (Fritz) Borah (a county commissioner), and Fred Dice. Only a few men in the second row are identified. Standing in the middle of the row in the dark suit is Adrian Reynolds, then Ellery Burford, and L. J. Borah. (ECHS; Lewis family collection.)

Rio Grande Railroad engineer Denny Cornwall was killed in this wreck at Eagle in January 1944. Witnesses reported that the train, carrying 300 troops, was traveling at a high rate of speed when the engine left the track, landing on its side after sideswiping a railroad toolhouse. Amazingly there were no other deaths or serious injuries. Below, the D&RG Railroad brought in a wrecker crew and special equipment to pull the 1700 Class locomotive engine upright. The baggage car followed the engine down the railroad grade, but the Pullman cars stayed on the tracks. (ECHS; Ping-DeGraw Collection.)

A crowd gathers at the Ping gas station to take a look at a recently killed mountain lion. There is still a mountain lion population in the hills surrounding Eagle. (ECHS; Ping-DeGraw Collection.)

Johnnie Robertson poses with the elk he killed in 1942. Robertson grew up on Brush Creek, and worked as a ranch hand. (ECHS; Ping-DeGraw Collection.)

Members of the Eagle River Valley Post No. 150 of the American Legion stage a Memorial Day ceremony at the Eagle Cemetery in 1940. The cemetery had not yet been landscaped. The Legion Post was located in Gypsum. (ECHS; Ping-DeGraw Collection.)

The Eagle Girl Scout troop prepares for a ceremony in the 1940s. Eagle has always been a town of civic organizations. Children could sign up for 4-H clubs or scout organizations. Adults had options ranging from civic groups, such as the Chamber of Commerce, to fraternal organizations such as the Masonic Lodge and Eastern Star. (ECHS; Ping-DeGraw Collection.)

Fred and Mary Rule ranched about 5 miles up Brush Creek, in the area where the Ridgway ranch is now located. The Rules raised cattle and potatoes and were active in 4-H and the County Fair. Above, the Rule sons Danny and Larry tend cattle on the family ranch. Danny Rule (below) took his grand champion Hereford heifer to the Colorado State Fair in 1940, winning a purple ribbon there. He then entered the animal in open class, going up against the best breeders in the state, and took first place. When offered $300 for the animal, he refused to sell. Dan continued to ranch as an adult and also worked as a banker, serving a stint as president of the First National Bank of Eagle. (ECHS; Ping-DeGraw Collection.)

Brush Creek rancher William Mayer started the first dairy in Eagle. In those early days, milk was delivered to homes in Eagle by a horse-drawn wagon (the wagon can be seen at the Eagle County Historical Museum). The milk was placed in narrow-neck glass bottles topped with cardboard caps. All of the milk was whole—it was up to the customer to let the cream rise then skim it off for other purposes, such as churning butter or ice cream. In later years, rancher Ross Chambers took over the business, named it "Castle Peak Dairy," and moved it across the river to his ranch (located about where the Burger King now stands, at the Interstate 70 interchange). Chambers built a processing plant introducing pasteurized milk to the community. (ECHS; Ping-DeGraw Collection.)

The Castle Peak fire lookout was built in the early 1900s and was used by the Forest Service until 1938. The lookout tower was located in an area that is prone to electrical storms. The tower was dismantled sometime in the 1960s. (ECHS; edited by Mike Crabtree.)

It was lightning that triggered this blaze on Castle Peak on Friday morning, September 22, 1944. Fire crews gather in a meadow as they prepare to fight the blaze. The fire scorched 1,500 acres of pasture and timber before firefighters were able to bring it under control. Forest Ranger Ben Rice took Forest Service crews to the blaze. Sheriff Murray Wilson was credited with bringing in a detail of about 60 soldiers from Camp Hale to help fight the fire and a troop of 150 soldiers from Fort Warren, Wyoming. Ranchers scrambled to move hundreds of head of grazing cattle out of danger. Men and boys from all over the county quit the harvest field to help fight the fire. (ECHS; photograph edited by Mike Crabtree.)

The details of the particular fire this Forest Service crew is preparing to fight are unknown. The upper photograph shows a crew unfurling a hose from a water pump that has been loaded into the back of a pickup truck. Below, a team of men works a two-man saw to fell a snag. (Bill Johnson collection.)

Mountain Sheep Eagle, Colo.

This photograph appeared on the inside cover of the 1928 Eagle High School yearbook. Although there was never a big population of bighorn sheep on Brush Creek, they were known to winter there. The animals could be found in the summer on New York Mountain, Fools Peak, at Nolan Lake, and in the Metheney Park area. The sheep population declined in the mid-1950s due to poaching and disease. Below, a hunting family shows off their big game trophies. Market hunters severely depleted elk and deer during the mining days in the early 1900s, but populations started growing again in the 1930s, when the Game and Fish Department began regulating hunting seasons. Still, many locals tended to observe "Farmer's Season" (they hunted any time they could get away with it). (ECHS; Ping-DeGraw Collection.)

There was skiing in Eagle long before Vail was developed. The earliest ski run was "Danger Hill," near the cemetery and below the water tank. A rope tow, driven by a converted Chevy chassis and engine, pulled skiers up the hill. A bigger, better hill was developed up Bruce Creek on the Gordon Whittaker ranch. Skiers could cruise the hillsides below the scrub oak. Ice-skating took place either on the river or on a dike-fortified rink in the town park. (ECHS; Ping-DeGraw Collection.)

The class of 1947 Eagle High School (EHS) basketball team was the first in the school's history to make it to state competition. Pictured above from left to right are (first row) Albert Haggart, Jimmy Rule, unidentified, Willard Wilson, and Nickie Palese; (second row) Stewart Poet, Bob Childers, Wayne Cowden, Bob Berger, Lynn Randall, and Coach Nick Buchholz; (third row) Walt Leiber, Neil Fessenden, Fred Foss, Bob Randall, and Larry Byers. After being beaten by Stratton in the first round, the Eagles fought their way back through the consolation bracket and came from behind to beat Strasburg for the State B consolation trophy. The EHS team lost only one conference game from 1944 through 1947. After high school, players could join a town team. At right, brothers Wayne and Lynn Randall pose in the town team uniforms. (ECHS and Randall family.)

Photographer Leonard Ping (middle) prepares to snap photographs of deer browsing in town. Leonard, who took many of the photographs that appear in this book, is standing on the porch of the Ping Hotel on Capitol Street. (ECHS; Ping-DeGraw Collection.)

Notes written on the back of this photograph indicate these gentlemen are working in White Quail Gulch on New York Mountain (near Fulford). They could possibly be a CCC crew working on a trail, or a group of miners and engineers exploring a mine. The Doctor Jackpot mine is in that area. (ECHS; Ping-DeGraw Collection.)

Since the little community of Eagle got its start in the 1880s, community leaders have worked hard to promote it. A 1912 brochure carried the motto, "Eagle—not the largest, but the best town in Colorado." That brochure also promised "new strength and vigor, new courage and inspiration come with the cool, crisp air, with the endless sunshine, with the perennial blue sky, and the inspiring view of the mountains." Community boosters in the 1940s, when this photograph was taken, were equally enthusiastic. A brochure at that time noted that Eagle was located "in the heart of one of the finest stock raising districts in Colorado," and promised "unexcelled opportunities for the vacationer and sportsman." Eagle has changed considerably since those days. Condominiums outnumber cows, and nobody grows potatoes on a commercial basis. However, many Eagle residents probably would stand behind that claim that Eagle is "not the largest, but the best town in Colorado." (Koonce family collection.)

BIBLIOGRAPHY

Brown, Sharon; and Dana Dunbar Kamphausen. *Brush Creek Memories*. Eagle, CO: Manuscript, ECHS Archives, Eagle Public Library, 1980.

Dice, Helen. *A Cup of Clear Cold Water: Life on Brush Creek*. Montrose, CO: Lifetime Chronicle Press, 1980.

Eagle Valley Enterprise. Eagle, CO: Newspaper archives, Eagle Public Library, 1898–1949.

Knight, MacDonald; and Leonard Hammock. *Early Days on the Eagle*. Eagle, CO: self-published, 1965.

Koonce, Harold W. *Rambling Recollections of Mid-Early Eagle*. Eagle, CO: ECHS Archives, Eagle Public Library, 1992.

Koonce, Harold W. *A Rambling Record of the Koonce Family of Eagle, Colorado*. Eagle, CO: ECHS Archives, Eagle Public Library, 1992.

Wolle, Muriel Sibell. *Stampede to Timberline*. Boulder, CO: Muriel S. Wolle, 1949.

ABOUT THE ORGANIZATION

Exploring Eagle County History:

The Eagle County Historical Society and the Eagle Valley Library District are partners in the effort to create a quality local history archive. The archives may be accessed on the second floor of the Eagle Public Library, located at 600 Broadway in Eagle. Browsers are welcome. Additionally, historic photographs, biographies, and records are available on the "Local History" tab of the library website (EVLD.org).

Explore Eagle County history at the Eagle County Historical Museum, located at 100 Fairgrounds Road in Eagle. Maintained by the Eagle County Historical Society, the museum is housed in the big white barn at Chambers Park (adjacent to the information center) and is open during warm weather months. Learn more about the resources and activities of the Eagle County Historical Society by visiting their website at eaglecountyhistoricalsociety.com.

Contributions of photographs or materials to the historical archives are always welcome. Contact the Eagle Public Library at evldlohis@marmot.org, or at P.O. Box 240, Eagle, CO 81631. Contact the Eagle County Historical Society at P.O. Box 192, Eagle, CO 81631, or e-mail echs_eagle@yahoo.com.

Visit us at
arcadiapublishing.com

www.ingramcontent.com/pod-product-compliance
Lightning Source LLC
Chambersburg PA
CBHW080623110426
42813CB00006B/1587